Garages and Carports

Garages and Carports

by Robert Scharff

Drawings by
Donald W. Holohan
G. Robert Mull

POPULAR SCIENCE BOOKS

HARPER & ROW

New York, Evanston, San Francisco, London

Copyright © 1980 by Robert Scharff
Published by Book Division, Times Mirror Magazines, Inc.

Library of Congress Catalog Card Number: 80-5207
ISBN: 0-06-090822-X

Manufactured in the United States of America

2131358

Contents

1 | Your Present Car Storage Situation

GIVE YOURSELF a garage or carport designed for maximum service—not only as a shelter for your car, but as a multi-use structure. It can provide the necessary added space for the storage of many items that are now overflowing the closet or overcrowding the basement in the home itself. Or, it can provide for any number of uses that will increase the everyday enjoyment of living. And here's a very important point to keep in mind: It costs approximately half as much to provide extra living area in the garage as it does to add an equal amount of space in your present home.

If you have a garage or carport, you don't have to worry about the problem of a shelter for your car(s). Or do you? Have you come home recently to a garage so cluttered with *junk* that you can't put the family buggy to sleep in its own home? An answer to this problem is quite easy to find. Carefully plan storage areas in the garage that will neatly store garden tools of all kinds, fertilizer, sporting equipment, off-season gear, swings, lawn and porch furniture, sleds, boats, bicycles. Or, it might provide storage space for hand tools, stationary power tools, ladders, paint and paint brushes, and other useful articles. Garage clutter—as well as storage problems—in the house itself can be solved by employing a carefully thought out storage plan.

The garage is an ideal location for a home workshop. It's also a good place to change the car's oil, make engine repairs, or remove minor dents. **Note:** When working in a garage, beware of carbon monoxide. This poisonous gas is exhausted by the engine when it is running. Allowing the engine to run in a closed one-car garage for only *three minutes* will poison the air so that it becomes dangerous to breathe. If run for longer periods, the air will become *deadly*. Therefore, *never* run an engine in a closed garage.

If you don't presently have a garage on your property, it should be rated *very* high on your home improvement list. Our car is the second biggest investment most of us make; our home, of course, is the largest. And when you consider that a garage or carport which shelters and protects this large car investment is relatively modest, it makes good sense to add one to your property. Not only does a garage protect your car from the body and chassis damaging effects of rain, sleet, hail, ice, snow, dirt, dust, and sun, but it safeguards the parts of the car itself from larceny. It also protects the car against damage by mischievous children and teenage vandals.

A well-designed garage or carport will enhance the looks and value of your property. It will increase the selling price if and when you wish to sell your

A garage can take some of the storage burden away from the house. (Above) The family's all-year-round sporting equipment can easily be stored in a built-in cabinet along rear wall of garage. This will free closets in house for other storage duties.

home. But before the plans for the garage or carport are too far along, you should refer to the building code in force in your locality. This is especially important where the garage is to be attached to the house since a few codes still require special fireproof construction to prevent or at least retard the spread of fire from the garage to other parts of the house. This may mean building the walls of concrete blocks or brick, with the ceiling of concrete or other nonburning material, plus the use of a fireproof or metal-clad door between the house and the garage.

FINANCING A GARAGE OR CARPORT. For many of the improvements in this book, "pay-as-you-go" financing is the only feasible way of paying for the work. But when adding a garage or carport to your property, or when converting a garage to living space and then adding a garage or carport, "pay-as-you-go" tends to drag the job out, resulting in inconvenience and perhaps additional costs. In such cases, monthly-payment financing is often the best, and only, way to go. Check your local banker on the type of loan that would be best for you.

2 | Making The Most Of Your Present Garage

THE GARAGE is an important and useful part of the home. Unfortunately, most of us don't take full advantage of it. Many of us keep the family car, a few tools, and some other "junk" there, but that's about all we use the garage for. If you presently don't use it as a "real" storage area, workshop, garden work center, or a place for the children to play on rainy days, then you're not getting the most from your garage. Let's see how you can remedy this situation.

STORAGE. Lack of storage is a problem in every home. With a little effective planning, a cluttered, catchall garage can be turned into a well-organized area that could relieve a great deal of the storage problems in the house. Your garage is usually either square or rectangular. But, since your car doesn't match this shape, there are vacant corners, spaces overhead, and room all around the car that can be used to store the thousand-and-one things left over from the scanty closet room of the house.

Shelves. Shelves are an easy way to turn wasted space into storage space in your garage. You'll need a plan, so ask yourself these two questions: **What** needs to be stored? **Where** can you "shelve" it? Between the studs? At eye level for often used items or high up for less used things? And don't overlook the possibility of adding hooks to shelf bottoms for hanging things to double the efficiency of the shelf.

There are many materials available for making shelves. They include 1-by-4-inch to 1-by-12-inch pine and Douglas fir boards, pre-cut particleboard, hollow-core slab doors of Philippine mahogany (lauan) for big utility shelves, and, of course, plywood. For safety, the brackets should be securely attached to the wall studs.

There are three types of commercial shelf brackets available that can be used to build garage shelves:

1. **L-brackets.** To install these steel shelf brackets, you simply screw one leg of the bracket to the wall stud and the other leg to the wood shelf. If the shelf is longer than 36 inches, you may need to install another bracket in the middle to prevent sagging.

2. **S-brackets.** Shelves installed with S-brackets give you the added advantage of having a "stop" at the end of each shelf so stored items can't fall off. They also make handy "dividers" on shelves to help keep things organized.

3

The three common types of commercial shelf brackets suitable for garages: (left to right) L-bracket, S-bracket, and adjustable.

All you do is mount one edge of the S-bracket to the wall, the other to the shelf. The bracket can also be conveniently used underneath the shelf.

3. **Adjustable brackets.** To install this type of bracket, mount the standard strips to the studs with screws, and snap in the shelf brackets at just the height you need. The proper size shelf board can then be set on the brackets.

If you wish, you can make your own shelf brackets. As shown here, it is possible to build three strong shelves, plus all the necessary brackets from a

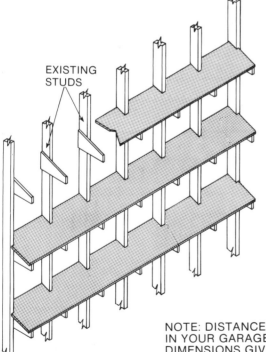

EXISTING STUDS

Shelves can be located between garage wall studs. A 4-by-8-foot sheet of 5/8-inch plywood will provide three strong shelves plus the support cleats.

NOTE: DISTANCE BETWEEN STUDS IN YOUR GARAGE MAY VARY FROM DIMENSIONS GIVEN—ADJUST ACCORDINGLY

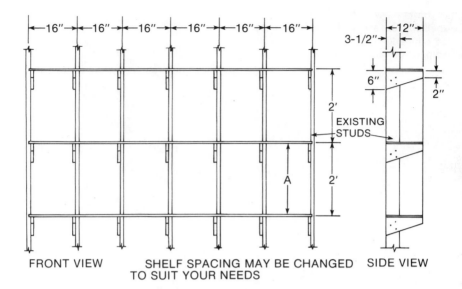

FRONT VIEW   SHELF SPACING MAY BE CHANGED   SIDE VIEW
                    TO SUIT YOUR NEEDS

There's nothing complicated about building between the stud shelves. In just a couple of hours, even an inexperienced do-it-yourselfer can install them, using a hammer and saw along with a few 6d or 8d common nails and white glue.

single sheet of 4-by-8-foot plywood. The thickness of these shelves need only be 5/8 inch. They are made as follows:

1. Lay out all parts on the plywood and then cut them to size.

2. On the sides of the studs, measure up from the floor to the desired shelf height and mark the support location on one side of each stud. Apply a wood glue to the stud below the mark and nail the support in place. Install all other supports in the same way.

3. Lay the shelf across the supports and mark the position of the notches around the studs. Cut the notches carefully with a saber saw. Then nail through the shelf into the supports.

4. Smooth the cut edges of the plywood and then seal or finish as you wish.

A free-standing shelf unit can also be used in a garage. This unit is built to stand against a wall, yet doesn't have to be fastened to it—the weight of the unit itself and the shelf load hold it firmly in place. Because it's not anchored, the whole unit can be moved to another location when your space requirements change.

To build a free-standing shelf unit, cut all parts to size from a 3/4-inch plywood panel. This includes the supports which are 6 feet long and the shelf supports which are 18 inches long. Glue-nail the plywood gussets to the upright supports. Then install the shelves. You can either permanently glue-nail the shelves to the supports or, if you expect to move the unit occasionally, you can use 1-1/2- or 2-inch flathead wood screws instead.

If you don't wish to paint the freestanding shelf unit, use a coat of water-repellent sealer on both edges and surface to minimize absorption of moisture from the air.

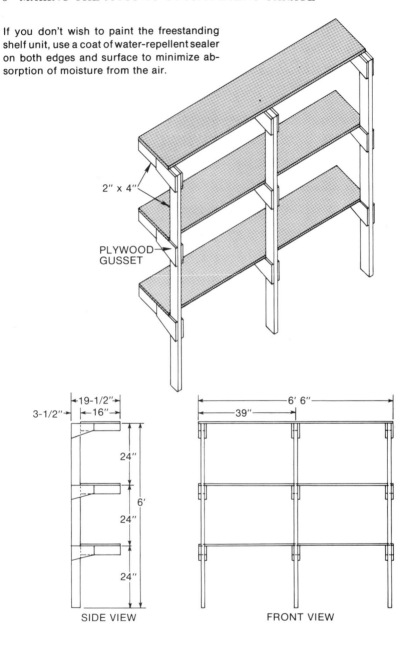

2" x 4"

PLYWOOD GUSSET

3-1/2" |←19-1/2"→| |←16"→| 24"   6'   24"   24"

SIDE VIEW

|←——6' 6"——→| |←——39"——→|

FRONT VIEW

Where the walls of the garage are open—the studs visible—innumerable small articles can be stored behind the outer level of these studs simply by making small shelves between studs, then setting a 1/4-by-1-1/2-inch strip along the outer edge to keep articles from sliding off the shelves. The variety of such shelves is almost endless, spacing between them determined by the items to be stored.

Shelves between the garage wall studs can be supported on cleats attached to the adjacent studs, spaced to meet storage needs, from the floor to the plate.

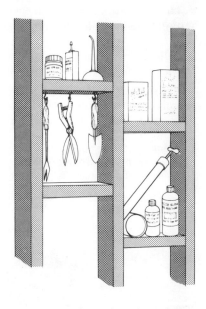

In some parts of the country, this "open" storage might well be objectionable due to dust accumulation or insect invasion. Covers of transparent plastic in the form of a weighted drop curtain will, in the majority of cases, handle this problem.

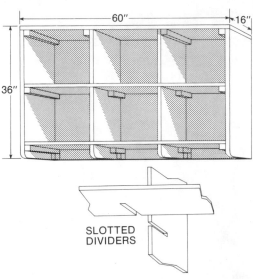

SLOTTED
DIVIDERS

This storage shelving unit can be made from two 4-by-8-foot-by-7/16-inch (or thicker) particleboard panels. Slotted shelves-dividers lock together to give the unit extra strength (Courtesy of Northwood Mills Ltd.).

Hanging storage units. An easy way to free up precious floor space in your garage is to use one of the new "hanging" systems available at your local hardware store. While there are several systems on the market, most involve the installation of some type of wall standards. These are usually channel shaped strips that attach to the wall surface studs. They are predrilled and generally come in lengths of 2 to 6 feet. These standards have vertical shaped slots in which the other component parts of the system can be positioned. Always remember that the heavier the load you want your system to hold, the closer

Hanging storage hooks and similar devices get tools, bicycles, ladder, screens, lawn equipment, etc. off of the floor of a garage and onto the wall. This will give any garage a neater appearance (Courtesy of Knape & Vogt Mfg. Co.).

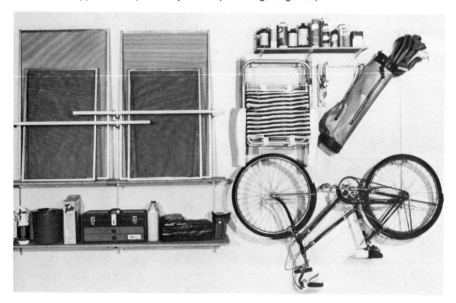

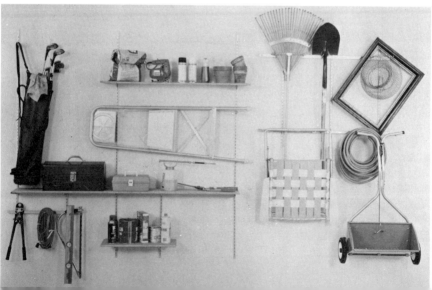

these standards should be spaced. The other components of the hanging system are all designed to integrate with each other to provide you with many storage options.

One of the most popular ways to accomplish hanging tool storage is by the use of perforated hardboard. The tools and similar items are hung on prefabricated metal hangers inserted in the perforations. This is a more flexible arrangement than using nails or wooden pegs, for example, because the hangers can simply be pulled from the holes and switched around as needed.

The 1/8-inch perforated hardboard is adequate when constructing panels for most small- and medium-sized hand tools and accessories. Heavy tools and equipment, such as shelves, ladders, crow bars, or garden type wheelbarrows, require the 1/4-inch size.

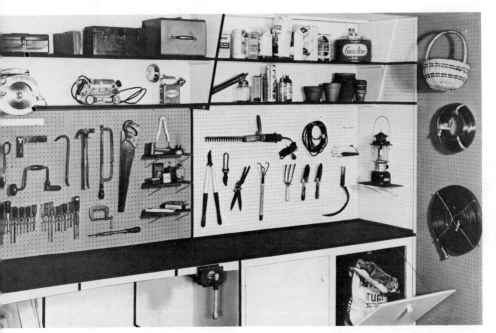

Perforated hardboard and its various uses can simplify many tool storage problems.

It's necessary to leave a gap between the perforated hardboard panels and the surface to which they are attached so that the hangers can be inserted through the holes. If the perforated hardboard is applied directly over studs, then there is plenty of space behind the board to insert the hooks. Remember to cut the panels into widths that equal a multiple of the center-to-center stud spacing, so that the edges meet and are attached to the studs themselves. For example, if a wall has studs on 16-inch centers, cut the 4-by-8-foot panels into 16-, 32-, or 48-inch widths. If you want to cover a complete wall, plan the placement of the panels before attaching them in order to avoid narrow pieces at the wall ends.

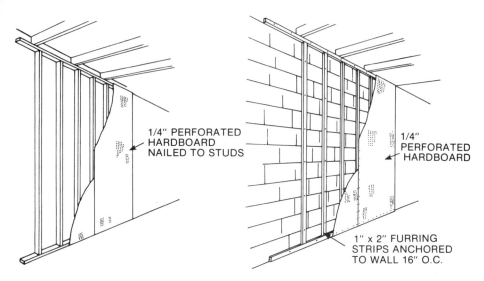

1/4" PERFORATED
HARDBOARD
NAILED TO STUDS

1/4"
PERFORATED
HARDBOARD

1" x 2" FURRING
STRIPS ANCHORED
TO WALL 16" O.C.

A method of installing perforated hardboard on a frame wall (left) and on a masonry wall (right).

If the walls of your garage are finished, you'll have to make special preparation. To begin with, a base frame must be built for the perforated hardboard to rest on. For example, if you plan to panel an entire wall with perforated hardboard, run 1-by-2-inch furring strips end-to-end along the base

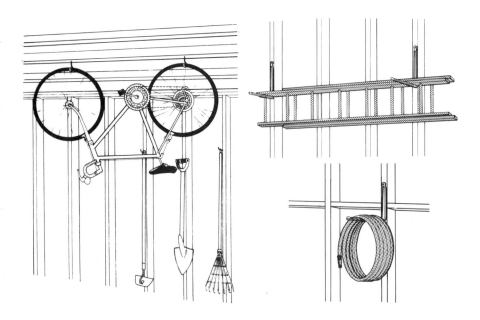

Screw hooks and L-shelf brackets provide an easy and neat way of getting things up and off of the garage floor.

of the wall, removing the baseboard if necessary. Follow this with a row of furring strips along the ceiling edge. Next, lay a row from the floor to the ceiling along both edges of the wall. Finally, place rows of furring strips across the wall at 2-foot intervals. The hardboard is then attached to these strips.

There are many different types of hangers for use with perforated hardboard. A plain, U-shaped hook can handle most types of wrenches, measuring devices, putty knives, wire cutters, and other types of hand tools. There are also elongated wire hooks for hanging a series of hammers or a plane. A set of circular wire forms can hold screwdrivers, chisels, awls, and so on. When buying hooks, be sure you buy the appropriate size (1/8-inch or 1/4-inch) for the board you are going to use. Stabilizers that go across the base of the hooks will prevent the hooks from being pulled out when the tool is removed.

Simple hardware can often solve some hanging storage problems. For instance, L-shelf brackets can be used to hang a ladder, or a single one makes an excellent hose rack. Round-bend and square-bend screw hooks can provide orderly storage arrangements for your shovels, rakes, brooms, mops, etc.

Bicycle storage. If you're caught up in the new trend in bicycling or your children have bicycles, chances are the bikes are taking up a bit of garage space when they're not being used. It is possible to hang them from the garage ceiling with round-bend screw hooks, or better still, build the hanging bicycle rack illustrated in this chapter which will keep two bikes safely stored, out of the way of cars and pedestrian traffic.

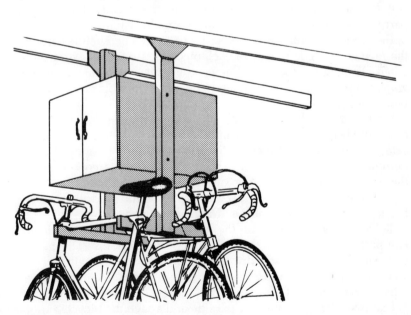

Park bicycles out of the way and gain a storage bonus with a single sheet of 5/8- or 3/4-inch exterior grade plywood.

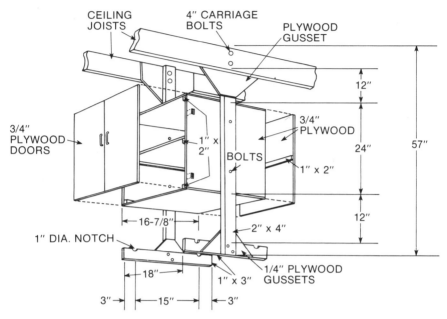

Construction details for the hanging bicycle rack. Dimensions may be varied slightly to fit the space available.

Before starting, measure the joist spacing to determine the size of the compartment and whether the bike supports should fasten on the inside or outside of the vertical hangers. Draw all parts on the plywood before cutting, placing the face grain the long way of each piece. Be sure to allow for the saw kerf when planning your layout. When cutting, place the panel face up if you're going to use a radial, table, or hand saw. For a portable power saw, place the panel face down.

Glue and nail 1-by-2 bracing to the compartment sides at the bottom and top and where the shelf will be installed. Glue-nail the bottom and top to the sides, nailing into the bracing. Place the shelf on the supports and install it permanently or not as you wish. Using 6d finish nails, countersink them, fill the holes with wood dough or surfacing putty, and sand smooth. Hang the doors. Brace or clamp the doors firmly in place and predrill the holes to guide the screws. Install door pulls and magnetic catches.

To be sure that the holes for the carriage bolts in the 2-by-4 hangers and the compartment match, drill the holes for one bolt first. Insert the bolt and tighten the nut down snug. Now drill the second hole through both pieces, assuring an exact match. Repeat for the other side. Use the same method in attaching 2-by-4s to the joists. Clamp the 2-by-4s in place when drilling the first hole.

Use two carriage bolts on each side and attach the bicycle support to the 2-by-4 hangers. With only one bolt, the support will tend to rotate when only one bike is on the rack.

Cut a 1-inch diameter notch in each side of both supports to hold the bicycle frames. To cut a half circle slot in the edge of the 1-by-3, clamp a piece of scrap lumber to the edge and drill through it, using the hole in the scrap as a guide to hold the bit in place when cutting the half circle.

A neat touch to protect the finish of the bike is to glue small pieces of carpeting or felt in the slots. If this is done, increase the slot size by 1/4 inch or 1/2 inch to compensate for the thickness of the padding. Another touch is to drill through the bicycle support to run a locking chain around the bike frame.

The overhead area. By far the largest space available is found in the gable roof garage—with a hip-roof structure second in line. Except for large multi-car structures where a small apartment may be built overhead (see Chapter 6), this space is often unused entirely. The fact that an apartment can be made there suggests the value of the space.

Where the overhead roof area is small, such as in a one-car garage, it's best to use short, shelf-like sections supported in part by the roof rafters. These storage areas can be reached from a short ladder.

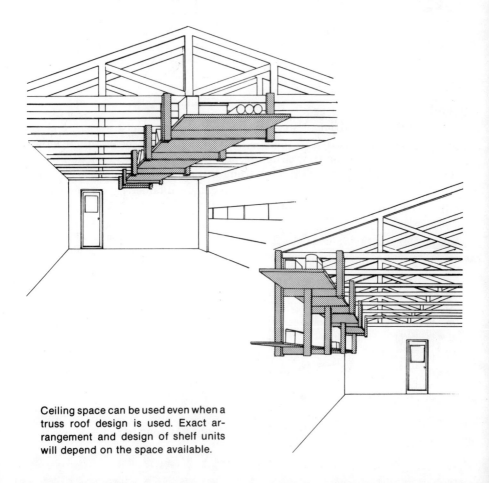

Ceiling space can be used even when a truss roof design is used. Exact arrangement and design of shelf units will depend on the space available.

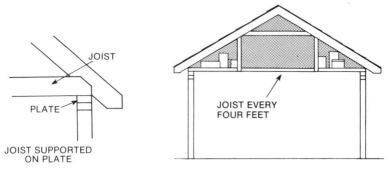

JOIST

PLATE

JOIST SUPPORTED
ON PLATE

JOIST EVERY
FOUR FEET

For a small, one-car garage where overhead storage space is at a premium, storage may be had by means of short shelf-like areas supported in part by the roof rafters. Reach these from a short ladder.

When the whole floor is built, support the joists on the top plate.

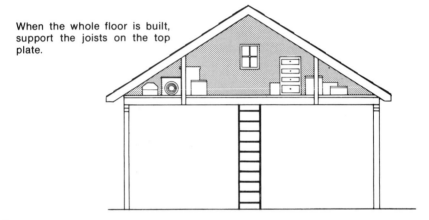

Where there is sufficient storage space available under the roof, a complete plywood floor can be installed. Add new joists, and support them either on the top plate (if the roof structure permits) or on blocks attached to the studs of the side walls. Additional strength for the floors can be gained by using rafter ties. Access to the storage area can be obtained by means of a disappearing folding attic stairway unit or a ladder.

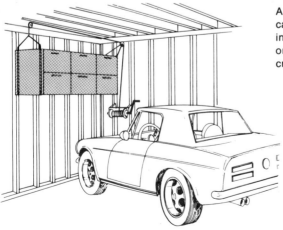

An easy-to-build storage box can settle the storage problems in many garages. It can be raised or lowered by means of a boat crank fastened to the wall.

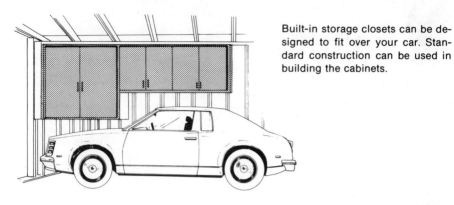

Built-in storage closets can be designed to fit over your car. Standard construction can be used in
building the cabinets.

Where roof trusses make access to the under-roof area rather difficult, shelves of various sizes and designs may be suspended and supported by the joists. The suspended members are usually 2-by-4s with plywood shelves. Commercial suspended storage units are available that permit you to tailor-make garage storage units to fit your needs. There are even units that allow you to store items over the hood of your car.

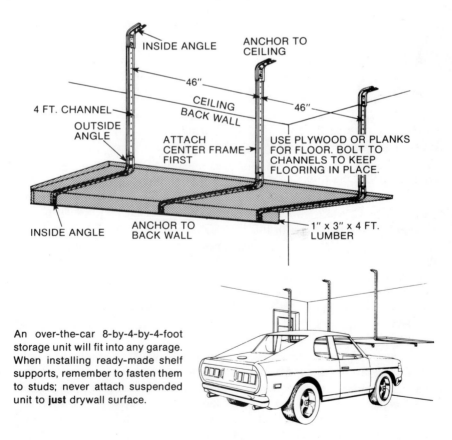

INSIDE ANGLE

ANCHOR TO
CEILING

46"

4 FT. CHANNEL

CEILING
BACK WALL

46"

OUTSIDE
ANGLE

ATTACH
CENTER FRAME
FIRST

USE PLYWOOD OR PLANKS
FOR FLOOR. BOLT TO
CHANNELS TO KEEP
FLOORING IN PLACE.

INSIDE ANGLE

ANCHOR TO
BACK WALL

1" x 3" x 4 FT.
LUMBER

An over-the-car 8-by-4-by-4-foot
storage unit will fit into any garage.
When installing ready-made shelf
supports, remember to fasten them
to studs; never attach suspended
unit to **just** drywall surface.

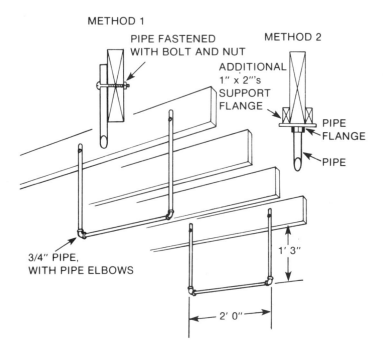

Overhead storage rack for storing lumber, storm windows, and screens. Made from 3/4-inch galvanized pipe, the rack's dimensions may be varied to fit your overhead storage needs. Two methods of fastening the pipe to the joists are shown.

WORKSHOP. The garage has definite advantages over the basement when it comes to a workshop location. For instance, it is a more convenient place to bring lumber and bulky supplies and, later, to remove finished projects. There is no maneuvering of big pieces around corners and up and down stairs. A garage will also have more unobstructed space. It has no posts, as in many basements, to interfere with the most convenient plan. Probably its biggest single advantage is that it is physically remote from the house itself (except in the case of built-in garages), allowing the rest of the family to remain relatively undisturbed by the noise a power tool can make. Of course, you must remember that your garage, if detached, is probably unheated and, to get all-year use from the shop, supplementary heating will have to be incorporated. Similarly, adequate lighting—a requirement for safety and accuracy—will have to be installed.

To economize on floor space, plan to use the wall for storage as much as possible, reserving the undercounter area for additional major tools. Regardless of how many you now own, be sure to provide for future expansion, as your needs and skills grow. It is really amazing how rapidly necessities accumulate. Somehow or other, each time a new project is undertaken, we seem to find a need for a tool that will make the new job easier or get it done faster and better. If you do any amount of auto repairs, you'll probably want to arrange your shop to handle this type of work.

The cabinets and built-in unit for a workshop shown here are thought stimulators only. Their size and layouts should be varied to fit your garage space. While 3/4-inch solid wood planking is illustrated, plywood or particleboard may be used. The construction would change only slightly.

The convenience of an orderly, well-planned workshop is an important asset when doing anything from building a simple bookshelf to making a major home improvement or when performing necessary maintenance and repair chores. The disorderly jungle of junk (above) can be changed into an orderly workshop (below) by careful planning and a little work (Courtesy of Western Wood Products Assoc.).

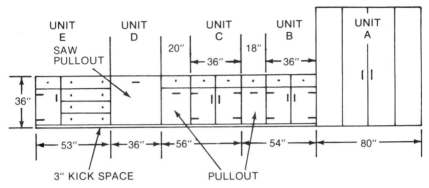

Typical side wall layout of garage workshop. Location and dimensions of unit can be varied to fit available space. Letters identify storage unit construction details.

A storage wall can perform other functions in addition to its workshop tasks. For instance, the large cabinet is planned for full ceiling use and to extend as deep as your space allows. It is divided into two basic sections, one for heavy, bulky items that can't be lifted from the floor, such as lawnmowers. Other garden tools—spades, forks, even a hose—can be kept here too, stored on hooks fastened around the interior surfaces. In the second section, the design is for shelf storage. Shelves can be made adjustable with standard hardware as here or can be fixed in place by cleats nailed to the cabinet sides. Although the adjustable hardware is the more costly method, it is preferred for the flexibility it allows. Actually, a most valuable feature of this section is the security compartment, where dangerous poisons may be stored under lock and key. Keep insecticides, weed killers, and other possible sources of trouble here, safe from inquisitive children. The lock may be of any type you find convenient. Even a simple hasp and padlock arrangement will do the job well.

Storage for lawnmower as well as other bulky objects is provided by the large cabinet in the corner of the garage. The doors are constructed of tongue-and-groove Ponderosa pine (Courtesy of Western Wood Products Assoc.).

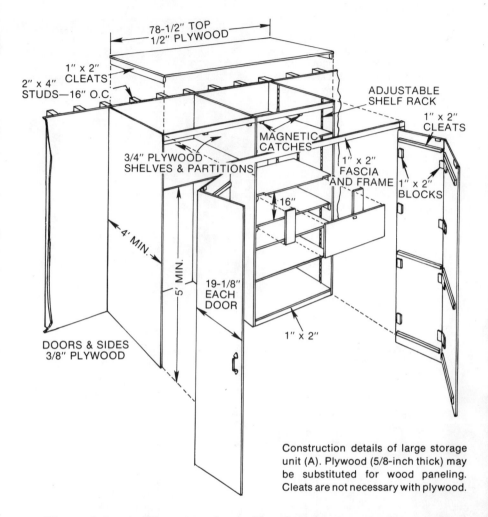

78-1/2" TOP
1/2" PLYWOOD

1" x 2"
CLEATS
2" x 4"
STUDS—16" O.C.

ADJUSTABLE
SHELF RACK

1" x 2"
CLEATS

MAGNETIC
CATCHES

3/4" PLYWOOD
SHELVES & PARTITIONS

1" x 2"
FASCIA
AND FRAME

1" x 2"
BLOCKS

16"

4' MIN.

5' MIN.

19-1/8"
EACH
DOOR

1" x 2"

DOORS & SIDES
3/8" PLYWOOD

Construction details of large storage
unit (A). Plywood (5/8-inch thick) may
be substituted for wood paneling.
Cleats are not necessary with plywood.

The workshop itself consists of a workbench and its associated storage features. The two sections adjacent to the ceiling-high storage cabinet are identical, although dimensions may vary from one to the other, depending on
one's purpose. Three types of storage are provided—pullout drawers, fixed
shelves, and a roll-away cart which, in the photo, is planned for paint and
painting tool storage. However, roll-aways can be used advantageously in
other ways, also.

With the proper arrangement of pegs, for example, you can neatly store
five or six portable electric tools and their accessories. Or, you can make a
roll-away into a portable workshop that goes to the job by fitting it out with
racks for small tools and a few compartments for nails, screws, and assorted
hardware. Other useful ideas to fit your special needs will occur to you. Of
course, if you need only one roll-away, use the space for the second for another
purpose—more shelves or extra storage drawers.

Paint storage cart uses adjustable shelf track for convenience. Place pegs at desired heights, gluing them in holes in back. Note that casters extend below kick plate.

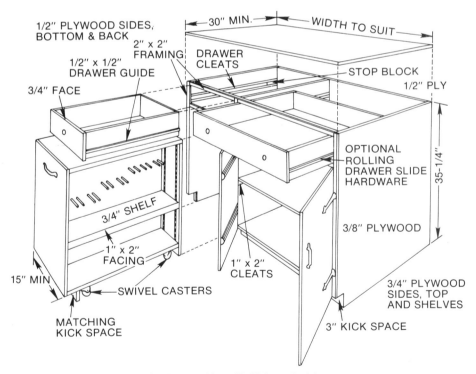

1/2″ PLYWOOD SIDES, BOTTOM & BACK

2″ x 2″ FRAMING

1/2″ x 1/2″ DRAWER GUIDE

3/4″ FACE

30″ MIN.

WIDTH TO SUIT

DRAWER CLEATS

STOP BLOCK

1/2″ PLY

OPTIONAL ROLLING DRAWER SLIDE HARDWARE

35-1/4″

3/4″ SHELF

1″ x 2″ FACING

1″ x 2″ CLEATS

3/8″ PLYWOOD

15″ MIN

SWIVEL CASTERS

3/4″ PLYWOOD SIDES, TOP AND SHELVES

MATCHING KICK SPACE

3″ KICK SPACE

Construction details of pullout-cabinet (B-C) in typical layout (page 18). Unit E in this layout is similar to B-C except that the widest part is a full-length drawer storage area, while portion occupied in B-C by the pullout is set aside for shelf storage.

When planning your garage shop layout, consider the stationary power tools you already have, as well as those you intend to purchase. The most basic is the table saw, already provided for in our scheme of things. The dimensions of this unit must be determined by the size of the saw table, unless your table

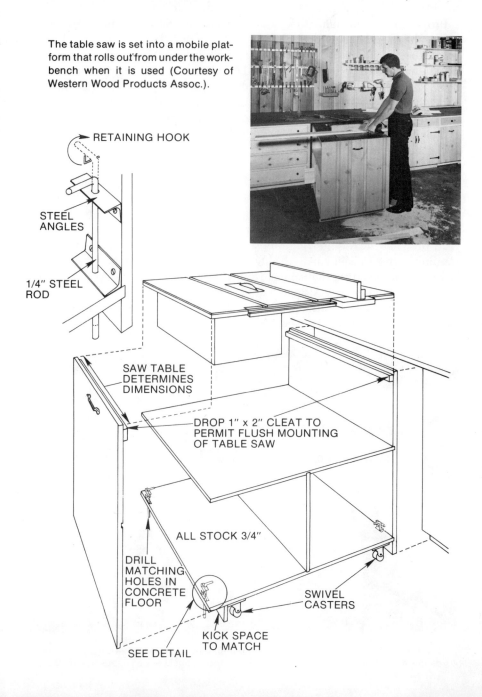

The table saw is set into a mobile platform that rolls out from under the workbench when it is used (Courtesy of Western Wood Products Assoc.).

RETAINING HOOK

STEEL ANGLES

1/4" STEEL ROD

SAW TABLE DETERMINES DIMENSIONS

DROP 1" x 2" CLEAT TO PERMIT FLUSH MOUNTING OF TABLE SAW

ALL STOCK 3/4"

DRILL MATCHING HOLES IN CONCRETE FLOOR

SWIVEL CASTERS

KICK SPACE TO MATCH

SEE DETAIL

is very small. Then, provision must be made to set the saw into a frame which is, in turn, placed on the top of the cart. Most heavy-duty saws will be large enough to mount directly. Use 3/4-inch plywood throughout, except for the facing, which is constructed of paneling. Rabbets are necessary, for extreme rigidity of the unit is a must if accurate work is to be done.

Provision must be made to lock the cart into position when the saw is being used. The drop latches for each corner can be purchased at your local hardware store or can easily be made. Size isn't critical. When fabricating your own latches, use 1/4-inch steel rod and bend them into the required shape in a vise. Then, mount them in angle brackets on the pullout unit. With the saw cart rolled out in working position, drop the latches down so that they rest on the floor. Mark the points of contact carefully, and drill matching holes at least 1/2-inch deep in the concrete. Now the latches can drop into these masonry sockets to secure the cart adequately. Take care not to make the holes too big, or they'll be ineffective.

With all the section cabinets built and in place against the wall, only the top of the bench remains to be completed. As with any other project, you have a choice of materials, although it's generally wise to use a combination of two. Cover all the cabinets with 3/4-inch particleboard. While considerably heavier than plywood, it is quite rigid and the surface is very smooth, requiring no sanding. Drive finishing nails through the top into the uprights of the sections below, countersetting the nailheads and filling the holes with plastic wood. Sand smooth when dry. Although not really necessary, a top of 1/4-inch tempered hardboard will provide additional rigidity and shock-absorbing capability. It can be cut to size and glued over the particleboard.

A drop leaf table on the back wall is an additional feature of this workshop. Three pieces are hinged, allowing the table to be stored against the wall (Courtesy of Western Wood Products Assoc.).

If your "work" in the shop is only done occasionally, you may need only a workbench rather than a complete setup. But, remember that a businesslike workbench starts off shop jobs better. The one shown stands on 2-by-4 legs, braced in the rear with a 1-by-6 and crosswise by 2-by-4s. A shelf across these provides storage space for portable power tools. The wide front apron makes the bench more rigid and gives you a place to clamp boards for planing edges. Cut it short at one end if you plan to mount a vise.

SIMPLE WORKBENCH

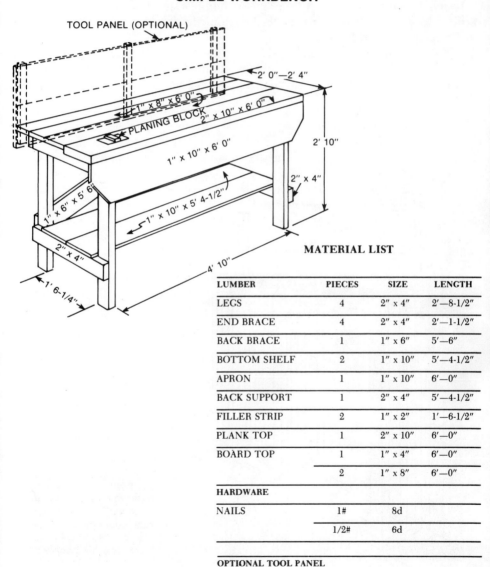

MATERIAL LIST

LUMBER	PIECES	SIZE	LENGTH
LEGS	4	2" x 4"	2'—8-1/2"
END BRACE	4	2" x 4"	2'—1-1/2"
BACK BRACE	1	1" x 6"	5'—6"
BOTTOM SHELF	2	1" x 10"	5'—4-1/2"
APRON	1	1" x 10"	6'—0"
BACK SUPPORT	1	2" x 4"	5'—4-1/2"
FILLER STRIP	2	1" x 2"	1'—6-1/2"
PLANK TOP	1	2" x 10"	6'—0"
BOARD TOP	1	1" x 4"	6'—0"
	2	1" x 8"	6'—0"
HARDWARE			
NAILS	1#	8d	
	1/2#	6d	
OPTIONAL TOOL PANEL			
BATTENS	3	1" x 2"	2'—0"
BOARDS	2	1" x 10"	6'—0"

The front of the working surface is a 2-by-10, recessed for a block that fits flush in one position or, when reversed, becomes a stop against which to butt stock for face planing. The thinner rear boards form a dropped surface where tools and other things will remain without rolling onto the work area in front. A tool panel can be fastened to upright battens. If it's made of perforated hardboard, you can use hook hangers in any desired arrangement.

POTTING BENCHES. A real worksaver for any home gardener is a potting bench. If you're only a "part-time" green thumb, a simple drop-leaf type that lifts up into place when you need the bench and folds out of sight when you're not using it would be ideal.

To construct the simple drop-leaf potting bench shown here, cut four holes—3, 4, 5, and 6 inches in diameter—in the 3/4-inch plywood, 4 inches from the end, 2 inches in from the front, with 2 inches between each hole.

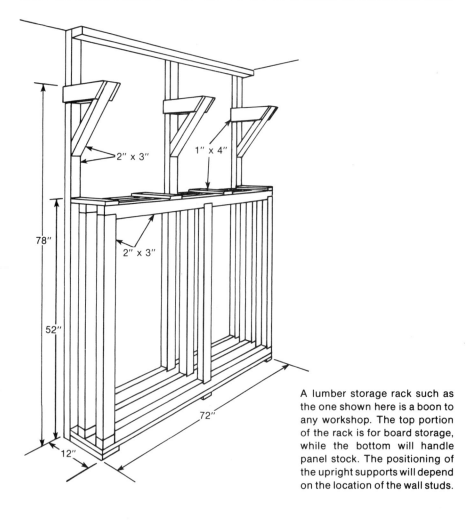

A lumber storage rack such as the one shown here is a boon to any workshop. The top portion of the rack is for board storage, while the bottom will handle panel stock. The positioning of the upright supports will depend on the location of the wall studs.

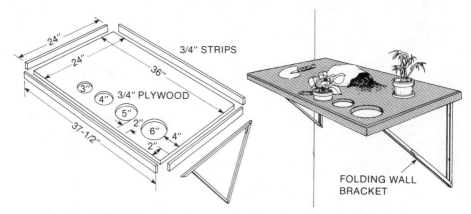

A simple potting bench like this lets you create a "gardening center" right in your own garage. Shelving above the bench could provide storage for pots, seeds, plant food, as well as other gardening items.

Glue and nail the lattice strip to the edges of the plywood, flush with the bottom to form a lip on the top surface. Sand all surfaces smooth. To complete, varnish it for a natural finish or paint it. Follow the manufacturer's directions enclosed with the fold-down brackets for attaching them to the plywood and wall.

If you're a "real" home gardener, you would appreciate the home-sized version of the professional nurserymen's potting bench illustrated in this chapter. Under the broad, table-height work surface, there's bin and cabinet storage, and above, lots of shelf space. To build this pro-type bench in your garage, proceed as follows:

1. With a large steel square, lay out the parts for the bench on 3/4-inch exterior-type plywood panels. Remember to allow for the saw kerfs when laying out the parts.

2. Assemble the unit back-side-down on the floor. Nail and glue the 2-by-4 flush with the back edge of the bench top. Then assemble the 4-inch wide strips on the cabinet bottom panel to make the base. Set the top and base up on edge to fasten the end and center standards.

3. Lift the bench into position against the wall and check to see that the base rests squarely on the floor. Then drive nails or lag screws through the 2-by-4 into the wall studs to secure the bench permanently.

4. After fastening a 1-by-2-inch doorstop to the underside of the bench top, hang the doors. Then build identical storage bins, which are simply open-topped boxes. Reinforce the corners of the bins with triangular corner blocks cut from 2-by-2s or 3/4-inch quarter round. Block the bottoms of the bins as required for the casters. Hang the doors using pin hinges.

5. Edge the front of the plywood bench top with a narrow hardwood facing. Then smooth off all of the joints, edges, and corners with a coarse or medium abrasive paper. After filling the nailholes and the exposed plywood edge grain with wood putty, smooth the entire assembly with fine abrasive paper.

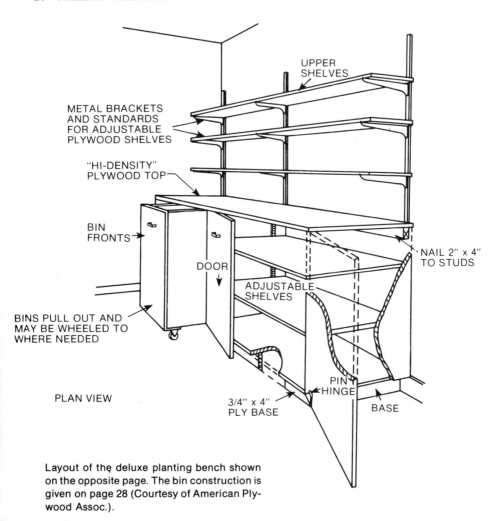

UPPER
SHELVES

METAL BRACKETS
AND STANDARDS
FOR ADJUSTABLE
PLYWOOD SHELVES

"HI-DENSITY"
PLYWOOD TOP

BIN
FRONTS

DOOR

ADJUSTABLE
SHELVES

NAIL 2" x 4"
TO STUDS

BINS PULL OUT AND
MAY BE WHEELED TO
WHERE NEEDED

PLAN VIEW

3/4" x 4"
PLY BASE

PIN
HINGE

BASE

Layout of the deluxe planting bench shown
on the opposite page. The bin construction is
given on page 28 (Courtesy of American Plywood Assoc.).

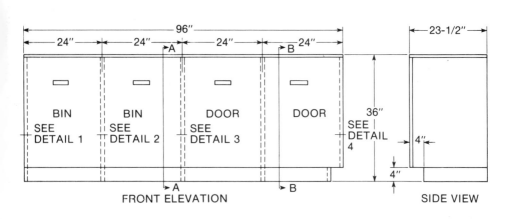

96"

24"   24"   24"   24"

23-1/2"

A   B

BIN   BIN   DOOR   DOOR   36"

SEE   SEE   SEE   SEE
DETAIL 1   DETAIL 2   DETAIL 3   DETAIL 4

4"

A   B

FRONT ELEVATION

4"

4"

SIDE VIEW

6. Give the unit and shelves one coat of house paint undercoat. Sand lightly, then brush on at least two coats of house paint or exterior trim enamel.

7. Arrange the brackets for the overhead shelves to suit yourself. Apply the standard metal pulls to the bins and doors. Install the friction door catches.

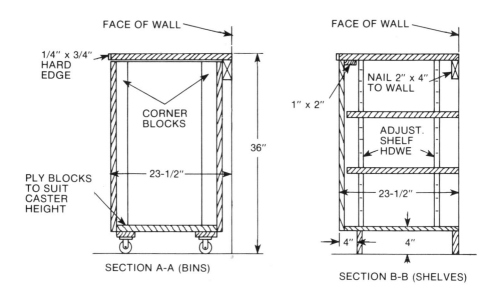

SECTION A-A (BINS)

SECTION B-B (SHELVES)

Construction details for the sliding undercounter bins and shelf storage areas. The close-up details show how the bins and doors fit into their respective portion under the counter. The doors, bins, and shelving may be painted or stained as you wish.

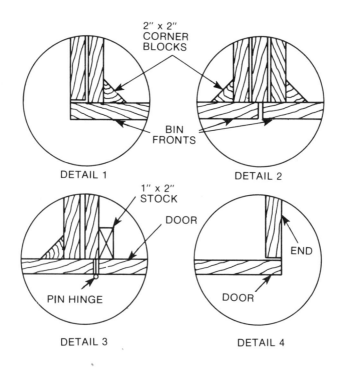

OTHER CONVENIENCES. Finishing touches will add further to the use of the garage. For example, finishing the bare studs or masonry walls with inexpensive paneling at once improves the looks of the interior and makes it easier to keep clean. While any type of paneling may be used, one of the most economical is hardboard. It can be applied to wall studs, if these are reasonably true and not over 16 inches apart. (If they are not, install inexpensive furring.) Use nails of a length that will penetrate the studding at least 1 inch. Start nailing panels in the middle, with the nails 8 inches apart. Then work out toward the edges, spacing the nails 4 inches apart along these and at least 1/4 inch inside the edge. Drive all nails perpendicular to the panel surface; never toenail into hardboard edges. Don't butt the panels tightly together, but simply bring the edges into contact.

If the garage is damp, use tempered hardboard. On concrete, cinder block, or other masonry walls, use masonry nails to attach vertical furring strips 16 inches center to center, shimming them up over low areas. Masonry walls must be completely dry, and exterior ones—those exposed to the weather on the outside—should be given an asphalt coating before any hardboard is applied. Don't carry panels all the way to the floor or ceiling, but leave a small gap at both for air to circulate behind the panels.

Painting the floor will also make the garage easier to clean and will make the structure more attractive. Use either a floor and deck enamel or a special concrete floor paint, as directed by its manufacturer on the container. The color selected is up to you. Also, keep in mind that you can paint game courts —such as hop-scotch and shuffleboard—on the floor for the children to use during bad weather.

Other conveniences that you'll want in the garage are water, heat, and electric power. With an attached garage this usually isn't a serious problem. Just connect into the house's existing system. The possible exception is the electricity. If you're adding a complete workshop, check to be sure that your present electrical service can handle the power tools. If not, a new circuit or service may have to be added. Information on adding heat, water, and electricity to a garage is given in Chapters 3 and 6.

Installing a door between the house and garage. It is usually desirable to have a door between the house and the attached garage. To install such an inside doorway, you must first make the opening in the wall. After selecting the position for the proposed door, you should determine the location of the studs. If possible, one side of the door should be located next to a stud. The width of the door will probably make it necessary to cut through at least two studs to the left or right. Using a plumb line, a long straightedge, and level, or a mason's level, draw an outline of the door at least 5 inches more than the height and 4 inches more than the width of the door itself. This allowance provides for the thickness of the door frame, for the shims or wedges by which the frame is set true, for expansion and door-swinging clearance, and for the finish floor, if laid after the doorway is framed. If the finish floor is already laid, deduct its thickness from the height allowance.

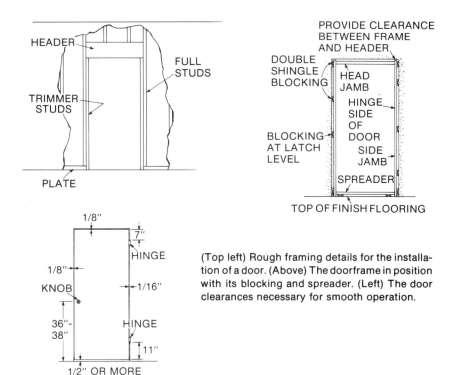

(Top left) Rough framing details for the installation of a door. (Above) The doorframe in position with its blocking and spreader. (Left) The door clearances necessary for smooth operation.

When cutting through a plaster wall, cut along the outline with a cold chisel or an old wood chisel and hammer. To prevent jagged edges, a long board or scantling can be lightly nailed along each line before chiseling. The horizontal line for the header is chiseled along the nearest interval between laths. After large starting holes are bored at the upper corners, a coarse compass saw or power saber saw should be used, since it will bend less than the ordinary handsaw when cutting across the laths down the vertical lines chiseled in the plaster. Check to be sure there are no electrical wires in the path to be cut. These vertical lines are continued down through the baseboard, and at the baseboard a handsaw is used. The lath and plaster within the opening can now be removed. The exposed studs are sawed horizontally across a level at their tops and pulled loose from their floor plate. If the plate is above floor level, it too must be sawed flush with the floor level.

Dry walls (plasterboard, wallboard, and paneling) are handled in much the same manner, except that chiseling isn't usually necessary. Rough openings are usually framed out to be 3 inches more than the door height and 2-1/2 inches more than the door width. This provides for the frame and its plumbing and leveling in the opening. Interior doorframes are made up of two side jambs and a head jamb, and they include stop moldings upon which the door closes. Some manufacturers produce doorframes with the door fitted and prehung, ready for installing. If you use one of these, purchase it ahead of time and measure it for accurate cutting. Application of the casing completes the job. When used with two- or three-piece jambs, casings can even be installed at the factory.

With the opening completed, the new framing, consisting of a double header and an extra stud at the side, is installed. Once the framing is completed, you're ready to install the doorframe.

When the frame and doors are not assembled and prefitted, the side jambs should be fabricated by nailing through the notch into the head jamb with three 7d or 8d coated nails. The assembled frames are then fastened in the rough openings by shingle wedges used between the side jamb and the stud. One jamb is plumbed and leveled using four or five sets of shingle wedges for the height of the frame. Two 8d finishing nails are used at each wedged area, one driven so that the doorstop will cover it. The opposite side jamb is now fastened in place with shingle wedges and finishing nails, using the first jamb as a guide in keeping a uniform width.

Casings are nailed to both the jamb and the framing studs or header, allowing about a 3/16-inch edge distance from the face of the jamb. Finish or casing nails in 6d or 7d sizes, depending on the thickness of the casing, are used to nail into the stud. Fourpenny or 5d finishing nails or 1-1/2-inch brads are used to fasten the thinner edge of the casing to the jamb. With hardwood, it is usually advisable to predrill to prevent splitting. Nails in the casing are located in pairs and spaced about 16 inches apart along the full height of the opening and at the head jamb. Casing used with any form of molded shape must have a mitered joint at the corners. When casing is square-edged, a butt joint may be made at the junction of the side and head casing.

The door opening is now complete except for fitting and securing the hardware and nailing the stops in proper position.

Double overhead garage doors. Sometimes, it might be well to consider the conveniences of having an overhead-type door at both ends of the garage. It's

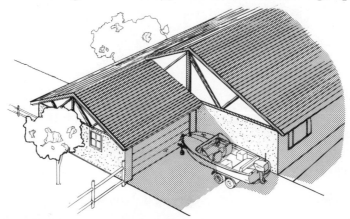

A double-ender garage is a great idea, especially for narrow lots.

a great idea to provide for throughway access from either end for moving a boat or camper to backyard storage, to make an enclosed patio or breeze-way of your garage, or to provide easy access to barbecue equipment, lawn furniture, mowers, and other items stored in the garage between the times they are used in the backyard. The double overhead doors are especially useful for narrow lots.

The installation of the framing and the overhead-type door is fully covered in Chapter 7.

3 | Adding An Attached Garage

IF YOUR house doesn't have a home for your car(s), consider adding an attached garage to the present structure. Remember that with the "right" attached garage, you'll add livability and convenience to your home and substantial resale value to your property.

The "right" attached garage for your home should be of the same architecture as the existing house. The new garage's roof should be of the same design and material as that of your home to keep a feeling of harmony. Also, to create a pleasing effect to the eye, have the roof of the garage parallel to the roof of the house, or nearly so. While it is usually best to use the same material in the construction of the garage as was used in the building of the house, this isn't a hard-and-fast rule. Frequently, a complementary, or even a contrasting, material will add interest to the overall design of your home and its attached garage.

Where to attach the garage to the house usually depends on the design of your home and the amount of property available to build the new structure. For instance, it's usually preferable to have the garage facing the side or back of the lot so that the garage interior won't be visible from the street when the big door is open. But, either of these locations need space, since they generally require a turning area.

An attached garage added to your home increases your property value and gives you greater convenience.

A garage attached to a breezeway offers many design possibilities.

Such problems as the location of the connecting door or breezeway between the house and the garage, and the part of the house into which the door or breezeway opens, must also be decided upon. Architects usually avoid having an entrance from a garage into the kitchen or dining room and prefer to locate it so that it opens into a hall or the living room. However, there is usually not too much scope in this matter when you are attaching a garage to a house that is already built. Probably the garage can be in only one or two places, and the location of the door or breezeway between it and the house won't be subject to too much choice.

The size of the detached garage is also determined by the location and space available. Keep in mind that the minimum size for a one-car garage is about 10- or 11-by-20 feet (some have been built smaller) and for a two-car garage about 21-by-20 feet. However, these sizes provide room for one or two cars, but little else. Since the average car is about 6 to 7 feet wide, minimum width doesn't leave much room at the sides. If you could add another foot or two, you'd have ample room for opening the car doors and you'd have some of the conveniences described in Chapter 2.

Pouring the concrete slab. The first step in building an attached garage is to outline the slab so that the site can be excavated for the foundation and floor. It's an easy job to square up the outline of the new garage with a surveyor's transit; but without it you can parallel one side or the back of the garage with the house by running cords and measuring carefully.

To square up the side of the garage with the existing side wall of the house, for example, it is necessary to mark off the location of the new structure in relation to the old. That is, measure the length of the garage against the house foundation and establish the two corners of the garage. (If possible, these corner points should line up with wall studs in the house.) Drive nails in the foundation wall at these two corner points. Attach a piece of twine or stout

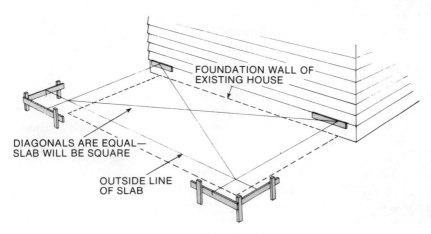

FOUNDATION WALL OF EXISTING HOUSE

DIAGONALS ARE EQUAL— SLAB WILL BE SQUARE

OUTSIDE LINE OF SLAB

Method of laying out the slab so that it is square with the house.

string to each of the nails and carry the string out past the desired location of the other side wall. Working with one string at a time, pull it taut and sight along the string to establish each of the wall corners. Then, drive a stake at each point and attach the cord to it so that it is accurately aligned with the house. To check the squareness of the house corner, measure 3 feet on the house wall and 4 feet on the string. Mark these distances and measure the straight-line distance between the two marks. This distance should be exactly 5 feet.

Once both of the house corners are square, measure the width of the garage along both strings and drive stakes at the proper dimensions. Then, run a string between the two stakes and check the corners to be sure they are square. To double check the garage area for squareness, run a string from corner to corner. When the dimensions are the same on each diagonal, the slab is square and parallel with the house wall.

After the corners of the garage have been located, three 1-by-3-inch or larger stakes of suitable length are driven at each location 4 feet (minimum) beyond the lines of the foundation; then 1-by-3- or 1-by-6-inch boards are nailed horizontally so the tops are all level at the same grade. String is next held across the top of opposite boards at two corners and adjusted so that it will be exactly over the nails in the corner stakes at either end; a plumb bob is handy for setting the lines. Saw kerfs at the outside edge are cut where the lines touch the boards so that they may be replaced if broken or disturbed. After similar cuts are located in all eight batter boards, the lines of the garage will be established. Check the diagonals again to make sure the corners are square.

Using the string as a guide, dig a 1-foot wide trench to a depth below the local frost line on three sides of the slab to act as a foundation for the floor; the house's foundation will serve that function on the fourth side. Check the local building department for advice on the depth of frost in your region.

Enough earth must be removed from the area to be occupied by the floor so that the ground will be 6 inches below the proposed floor level. Fill this floor area with 6 inches of cinders or gravel. Roll or tamp it down firmly so that footsteps will not show when the area is walked on. A lawn roller can be used for this job. Level the cinders or gravel with a carpenter's or mason's level as a guide. Boards should then be set against the stakes around the outside of the trench as the upper part of the concrete form for the walls. While the exact height of the floor will depend on the house's foundation, usually 4 inches above the ground level is sufficient.

The concrete is poured to form, in one mass, the foundation walls and floor. The finished surface is leveled off with a strikeboard and then smoothed with a level float. For a gritty, nonskid surface, finish with a wood float. For a smooth surface, use a steel trowel. It's important that the finishing be done after the concrete has become quite stiff. After the finishing is completed, the anchor bolts or clips should be set in the concrete. In colder climates, it is frequently a good idea to pour the foundation and slab separately. When doing this, an isolation or expansion joint is needed to relieve any possible stress between the foundation wall and the floor slab. This joint consists of a premolded strip of fiber material that extends the full depth of the slab or slightly below it. It need not exceed 1/2 inch thickness, and in most instances, 1/4 inch is sufficient. Some building codes still require that the foundation wall be poured on a footer.

The most convenient and economical source of concrete is a ready-mix producer. Full details on ordering and using ready-mix concrete can be found in Chapter 9. But, when pouring a slab for an attached garage, remember that special care should be used to secure a good joint where the new wall abuts against the old. If the walls are poured concrete, reinforcing rods may be set into the old walls and the new walls poured around them to bind the two walls together. With concrete blocks, it may be desirable to remove two or three from the old wall and set in new ones so that they are half in the old and half in the new wall. This firmly ties the two walls together. Reinforcing rods can also be used here. The outside of the joint should be carefully plastered and tarred so that it is well sealed and will not allow water to seep through and into the house.

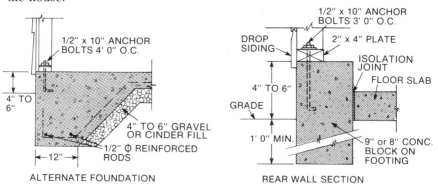

Two methods of pouring the slab: (left) integral footing-slab poured at one time; and (right) a slab and footing poured separately.

Walls for the attached garage. The base or sole plate goes on top of the foundation slab after it hardens; this usually takes about two or three days. It is held in place by anchor bolts or clips. (If anchor bolts are used, the plate will have to be drilled to accommodate them.) The studs are nailed to the plate or held in place by framing clips. To install the latter, bend the slotted angle to suit your needs, then nail in place with barbed nails. The studs may be placed 16 or 24 inches on centers, depending on local building code regulations. If the wall is to contain a window, don't try to frame the complete window, but merely nail the upper cripples (short studs) and upper trimming header in place. The upper trimming header is made of two 2-by-4s set on edge and placed side by side. Then, after the wall framing is up, the framing around the window can be completed by nailing in the lower trimming header, cripples, and side trimmers.

When a wall has been framed, set the lower ends of the studs against the lower plate and raise the assembly. This is usually a two-man job, since the framing for even one garage wall is bulky and heavy. Then, the lower ends of the studs should be toenailed into place on the lower plate. As mentioned earlier, framing clips may be used instead of toenailing.

Proceed to frame and erect the other two walls in the same manner. The upper trimming header above the garage door should be made of two 2-by-6s for 7- or 8-foot wide doors or 2-by-10s for 16-foot doors (instead of 2-by-4s) set on edge and placed side by side. This additional strength is required because of the wide door span. As the second wall frame goes up, toenail the two upper plates together where they abut. After all three wall frames are in place, nail on the top 2-by-4 plate, overlapping it to secure a rigid tie-in between the walls. During this job, check the walls for plumbness with a carpenter's level, and make sure that everything is straight and square before nailing on the top plates. The framework that adjoins the home should be fastened to the house's wall studs or frame with nails, lag screws, or anchor bolts. As described in Chapter 2, a doorway can be constructed between the house and newly attached garage.

Completing the job. Joists and rafters should be put up next. Run 2-by-4 ceiling joists, every 48 inches, between the side walls, toenailing them to the top plates with 10d nails. Use a 2-by-6-inch ceiling joist against the existing structure, and fasten it to both of the garage's top plates as well as the house's studs. The top edges of the joists are cut off flush with the top edges of the rafters once the rafters are in place.

The style of roof employed for the attached garage should either be the same as that of the house or at least complement it. The finished roof itself should also be the same color as the remaining portion of the house. If you're installing a gable roof, cut the 2-by-6-inch roof rafters to length, with the proper angle cut at the ridge and eave and with notches provided in the plates. Install the home side rafters first, nailing them to the house's studs, the garage's plates, and to the ridge. After the first rafters are in place, the roof is put up as described in Chapter 8. The installations of other roof designs are also

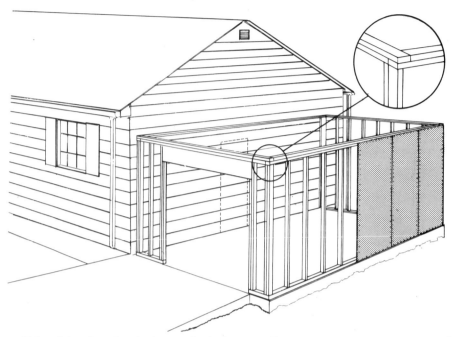

Sidewall framing of a single-car attached garage. Dotted line shows the possible location of a door into the house.

mentioned in that chapter. Remember that it is most important to use flashing between the old and new structure to prevent any water seepage into the house.

After the roof is completed, the siding can be installed. If exterior-grade plywood, paper-overlaid plywood, and similar sheet materials are used for siding, they are usually applied vertically. When used over sheathing, plywood should be at least 1/4 inch thick, although 5/16 and 3/8 inch will normally provide a more even surface. Hardboard should be 1/4 inch thick, and materials such as medium-density fiberboard should be 1/2 inch. All nailing should be over studs, and total effective penetration into wood should be at least 1-1/2 inches. For example, 3/8-inch plywood siding over 3/4-inch wood sheathing would require about a 7d nail, which is 2-1/4 inches long. This would result in a 1-1/8-inch penetration into the stud, but a total effective penetration of 1-7/8 inches into wood. Plywood should be nailed at 6-inch intervals around the perimeter and 12 inches at intermediate members. Hardboard siding should be nailed at 4- and 8-inch intervals. Joints of all types of sheet material should be caulked with mastic unless the joints are of the interlapping or matched type or battens are installed. A strip of 15-pound asphalt felt placed under uncaulked joints is good practice. Drop siding, wood shingles, or other similar materials may be substituted for plywood or hardboard, especially if they better match the style of your house.

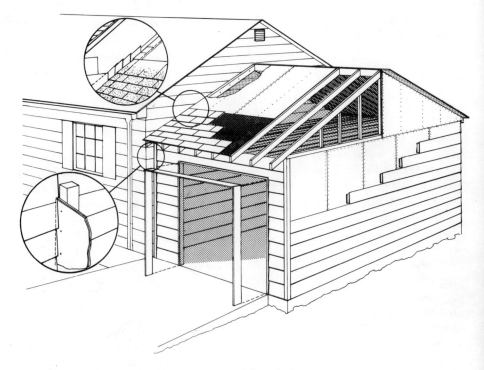

Attached garage with the finishing material applied.

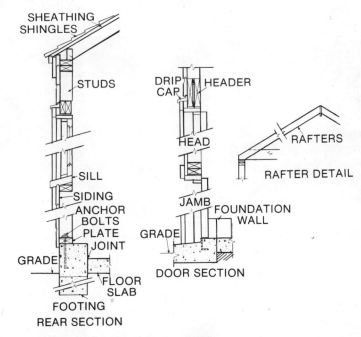

SHEATHING
SHINGLES

STUDS

DRIP
CAP

HEADER

HEAD

RAFTERS

RAFTER DETAIL

SILL

SIDING
ANCHOR
BOLTS
PLATE
JOINT

JAMB

FOUNDATION
WALL

GRADE

GRADE

DOOR SECTION

FLOOR
SLAB

FOOTING

REAR SECTION

Rear wall, door elevations of the attached garage.

It's often possible to carefully remove the siding on the garage-enclosed portion of the house and use it as part of the garage's siding. But, under certain local building or fire codes, it is necessary to install 1/2-inch gypsum board on the garage-house wall for fire protection. Check your local codes on this matter.

To select and install an overhead garage door, follow the information given in Chapter 7.

Other considerations. When planning your attached garage—or any garage as a matter of fact—lighting and ventilation are important considerations. One overhead light fixture is minimum. In addition, lights could be installed over the workbench, in the cupboard, on the balcony, or in connection with other special features that you have incorporated. You may also wish to install a floodlight in front of the garage so that the driveway or turning area can be lighted on dark nights.

At least one window is desirable to serve both as a source of light during the day and as ventilation. Ventilation of the garage is a necessity, particularly if the engine is operated inside the garage for any length of time (see page 1).

If the garage workshop is to be used all the year round, the garage should be insulated and provision should be made for heating it. It is often possible to heat it from the house heating system by running a warm-air duct, hot-water, or steam pipe from the house. Or, a separate heating unit, such as a small wood/coal-burning stove or other auxiliary heater, can be installed.

Kerosene heaters, either of the portable type or of the window type, are an excellent source of heat for garages (Courtesy of Koehring-Atomaster Div.).

4 | Extending Your Present Garage

IF YOUR present garage is too small, there are several ways to extend your present structure's usable space. You can convert it from a single-car unit to a double, add a "mini-garage," or attach an add-on shed. Of course, one of the simplest ways, as described in the previous chapter, is to add a carport as an additional garage-type shelter.

CONVERTING A SINGLE-CAR GARAGE TO A DOUBLE. One of the simplest ways to remedy the "too small" garage problem is to convert your present one-car structure into a two-car affair. This task is very similar to that of attaching a garage to a house (see Chapter 3). In fact, you're really attaching a garage to a garage.

The first step in the conversion job is to remove the trim siding, sheathing, windows, and doors from the side of the finished garage where the attachment is to be made. Do this job carefully as many of the materials may be reused in completing the project.

If you have the space at the side of your property, it's not too big a job to convert a single-car garage into a double (Courtesy of Frantz Mfg. Co.).

The next step is to pour the slab for the new portion of the garage. It should be made the same thickness as the old and tied to it with reinforcing rods. These rods should be set into both the new and old sections and concrete poured around them to tie the two floors together. Any large cracks or separations can be treated as a concrete repair (see page 150). To give a continuous floor effect, screed a thin coat of the new cement over the old portion. To effect a bond between the two concrete surfaces, use a cement adhesive or bonder as directed by the manufacturer. This can be accomplished after the two garages are joined together.

The framework for three walls and the roof structure is completed in the same manner as when attaching to a house; no studs are needed for the wall that adjoins the old garage. The corner studs, ceiling joists, and roof rafters where the two structures are to be joined should be fastened together with lag screws. This will mean that there will be double corner studs, ceiling joists, and roof rafters where the two garages meet. The wall studs and bottom plate of the old portion of the garage can now be removed. An adjustable floor jack post should be placed in the center of the double ceiling joists and should be tightly secured to help support the roof load.

Sheathing for the roof and sidewalls is nailed in place on the new garage. Then the finish roofing and siding, which match the house or the old garage, are added. For details, see Chapters 3 and 6. Once the trim and overhead door are installed, you'll have a two-car garage instead of one.

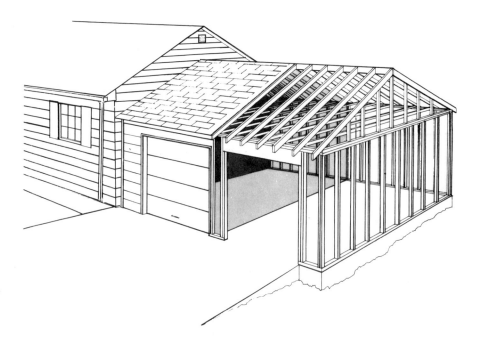

Framing details for attaching a garage to a garage.

GARAGE ADD-ONS. One of the easiest ways to forever end the extra work of hauling garden supplies out of the basement, without letting them clutter up your garage, is to construct an add-on storage building. This structure can range from a simple lean-to that can be tucked under a wide roof overhang or built onto a garage with its own roof extension to a mini-garage for handling both bicycles and garden equipment. It's also possible to add some extra features in a simple lean-to building.

Outdoor storage and dining lean-to. This add-on shed was designed to be a multipurpose unit. The shed has a spacious well-planned barbecue cupboard that holds pots, pans, and utensils, as well as a table that folds down to provide table space for four or more people. In addition to this dining facility, there are two perforated hardboard-lined walk-in closets that can solve all of your outdoor storage problems. The smaller closet has enough space to accommodate all of your garden tools and equipment, including the lawnmower. The larger closet is just right for storing extra tables and chairs and any other items that may need protection from the weather. The removal of such items from the garage will make it appear to be bigger.

In warm climates, where frost-heaving of the ground is never encountered, the shed may be built directly on a 3-inch concrete slab poured over a bed of gravel. In colder areas, particularly where heavy snows occur, the outside walls of the shed must be supported on a foundation which extends down to the frost line. This is rarely more than 30 inches below grade. Check with your local building department if you're not sure of the proper depth in your area. On basementless houses you can arrive at the proper depth by making the new foundation as deep as the existing house foundation. Dig alongside the house foundation until you reach the bottom of the footing, then extend this excavation out along the lines of the outside shed walls. After the concrete foundation and 3-inch-thick slab have been poured, insert anchor bolts for the sill plates before the concrete hardens. Allow the concrete to cure for three or more days; coat the joint between the old and new foundations with a mastic waterproofing compound.

This multipurpose storage add-on will give you many days of outdoor dining (Courtesy of Masonite Corporation.).

Start the framing by fastening all of the sill plates to bolts that were embedded in the concrete before it hardened. Next, nail the 2-by-4 horizontal rafter support and the 2-by-2 studs to the garage wall. If your garage has clapboard or shingle siding, fasten a clapboard filler to the siding to provide a flat nailing base for the 2-by-4 rafter support. Frame the remaining outside walls of the shed and then nail on the rafters. Face the rear wall of the shed with hardboard and perforated hardboard before you start the interior framing for the table and counter. After all framing has been completed, nail on the roof sheathing, the 1-by-6 fascia board, and the hardboard siding. Insert the edge of the siding into a vertical 1/8-inch saw kerf cut into the garage siding with a portable circular saw. Caulk this joint to make it waterproof.

Complete the roof by tacking the tarpaper over the sheathing and nailing shingles over this to match the shingles on the roof of the garage. A length of copper or plastic roof flashing slipped under the house siding and over the new shingles will make this roof-to-wall joint waterproof. Fasten the flashing in place by driving aluminum nails through the siding. Install the roof gutter by nailing the supporting strap-hangers directly to the roof sheathing, under the shingles.

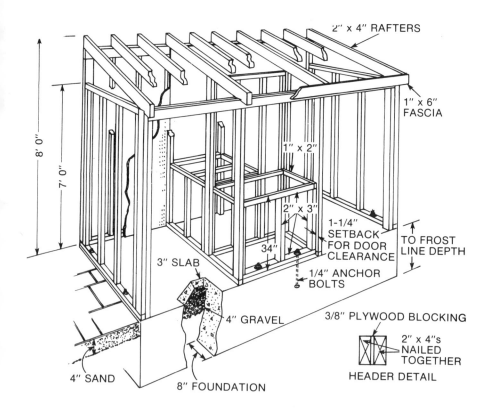

Construction details for multipurpose storage unit.

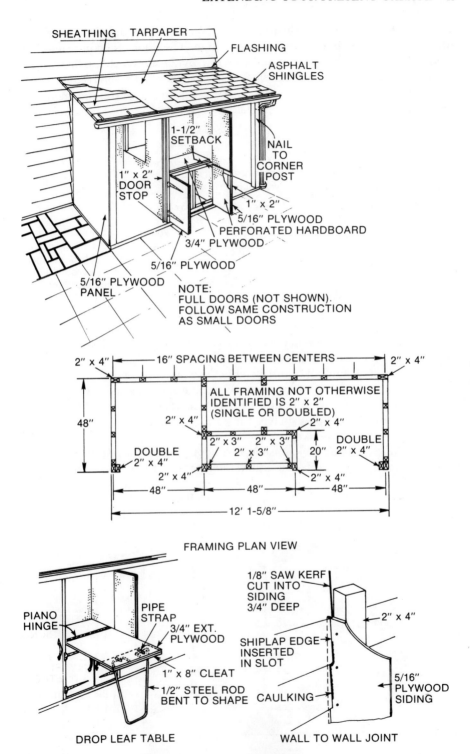

SHEATHING   TARPAPER

FLASHING

ASPHALT
SHINGLES

1-1/2"
SETBACK

NAIL
TO
CORNER
POST

1" x 2"
DOOR
STOP

1" x 2"

5/16" PLYWOOD
PERFORATED HARDBOARD

3/4" PLYWOOD

5/16" PLYWOOD

5/16" PLYWOOD
PANEL

NOTE:
FULL DOORS (NOT SHOWN).
FOLLOW SAME CONSTRUCTION
AS SMALL DOORS

2" x 4"   16" SPACING BETWEEN CENTERS   2" x 4"

ALL FRAMING NOT OTHERWISE
IDENTIFIED IS 2" x 2"
(SINGLE OR DOUBLED)

2" x 4"   2" x 4"

48"

2" x 3"   2" x 3"   DOUBLE
2" x 3"   2" x 4"

DOUBLE
2" x 4"   20"

2" x 4"   2" x 4"

48"   48"   48"

12' 1-5/8"

FRAMING PLAN VIEW

PIANO
HINGE

PIPE
STRAP

3/4" EXT.
PLYWOOD

1" x 8" CLEAT

1/2" STEEL ROD
BENT TO SHAPE

1/8" SAW KERF
CUT INTO
SIDING
3/4" DEEP

2" x 4"

SHIPLAP EDGE
INSERTED
IN SLOT

5/16"
PLYWOOD
SIDING

CAULKING

DROP LEAF TABLE

WALL TO WALL JOINT

Line the interior of the shed with hardboard panels, and then attach the drop-leaf table with a length of piano hinge. The doors are constructed by nailing and gluing the hardboard panels to 1-by-2 frames. Attach these doors with strap hinges. The door handles, cupboard door locks, and friction catches go on next. The last step is to trim all of the exposed door framing members with strips to match the doors and siding.

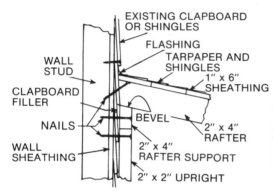

EXISTING CLAPBOARD OR SHINGLES
FLASHING
WALL STUD
TARPAPER AND SHINGLES
1" x 6" SHEATHING
CLAPBOARD FILLER
BEVEL
NAILS
2" x 4" RAFTER
WALL SHEATHING
2" x 4" RAFTER SUPPORT
2" x 2" UPRIGHT

Typical roof to wall joint. It is suitable for add-on buildings as well as for attached garages. Plywood can be substituted for 1-by-6-inch roof sheathing.

Add-on sheds don't have to be this big or encompassing. For instance, a carefully planned 3-foot deep lean-to can provide ample floor space for power mowers, wheelbarrows, and even barbecues. To accommodate these items, however, the doors must be able to swing wide enough to admit the equipment. A vital part of any narrow storage shed is a tall revolving rack capable of providing hanging space for long-handled tools, fishing poles, and other sporting goods, plus shelves for potting materials, paints, work shoes, wading boots, and the like.

To build a revolving rack, push in a wooden plug for the bottom rack pivot when pouring the concrete slab. Build rack frames of 1-by-2s faced with perforated hardboard. Bolt them to a 2-by-2-inch mast for the revolving rack. Grease the pivot dowels liberally when installing them.

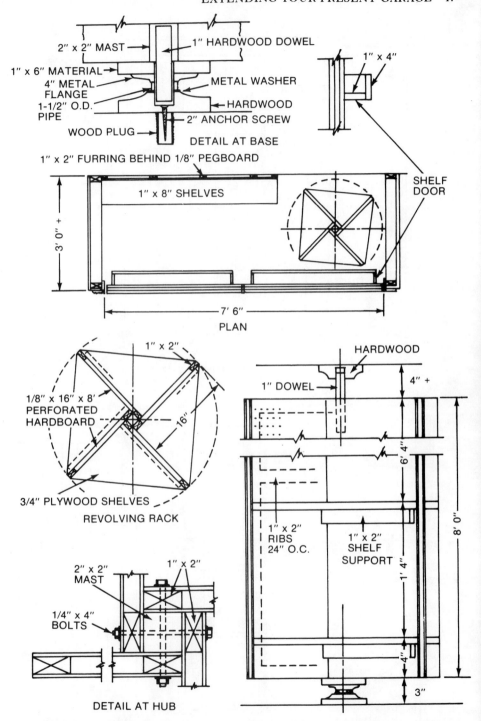

2" x 2" MAST
1" HARDWOOD DOWEL
1" x 6" MATERIAL
4" METAL FLANGE
1-1/2" O.D. PIPE
METAL WASHER
HARDWOOD
2" ANCHOR SCREW
WOOD PLUG
DETAIL AT BASE
1" x 4"

1" x 2" FURRING BEHIND 1/8" PEGBOARD
1" x 8" SHELVES
3' 0" +
SHELF DOOR
7' 6"
PLAN

1" x 2"
1/8" x 16" x 8' PERFORATED HARDBOARD
16"
3/4" PLYWOOD SHELVES
REVOLVING RACK

HARDWOOD
1" DOWEL
4" +
6' 4"
8' 0"
1" x 2" RIBS 24" O.C.
1" x 2" SHELF SUPPORT
1' 4"
4"
3"

2" x 2" MAST
1" x 2"
1/4" x 4" BOLTS
DETAIL AT HUB

Details for the location and construction of the revolving rack that gives so much storage space to the small add-on.

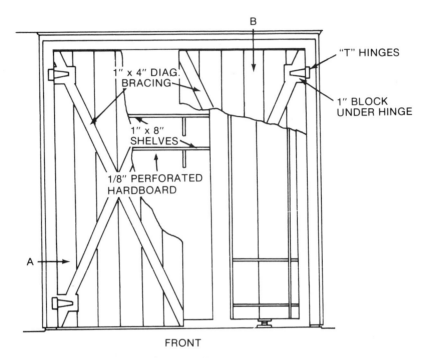

B

"T" HINGES

1" x 4" DIAG.
BRACING

1" BLOCK
UNDER HINGE

1" x 8"
SHELVES

1/8" PERFORATED
HARDBOARD

A

FRONT

Construction details for the small storage add-on.

DETAIL A

EXISTING SOFFIT

1/4" RD.

2" x 6"

TYPICAL
TRIM

BLOCKS—24" O.C.
2" x 6" MATERIAL

1" x 3"

DETAIL B

SIDING

2" x 4"
FRAMING

6" MIN.

DETAIL C

1" x 6"

1" x 4"

3' 9"

1" x 8"

C

BACK   FRONT

SECTION

DOOR

Mini-garage. Here is a solution to the overflowing-garage problem—a shipshape addition you can build onto the right or left side of a garage. Never more need you stumble over the power mower or open the car door against a jumble of bikes and long-handled tools. Separate doors open onto three compartments, one for bicycles, a center one for mowers, spreaders, and other big gardening equipment, and a small end storage room for fertilizer, small tools, and potting supplies.

Pour a concrete slab about 5-by-18 feet with suitably deep footings and low sills for the new walls. Set in bolts for the 2-by-4-inch sill plates. Erect 2-by-4-inch studs, doubled at corners, with doubled 2-by-4 plates across at the top. Remove the fascia board from the garage roof so that you can nail new rafters to the old. Choose new siding, trim, roofing, and finish to match or harmonize with the main structure.

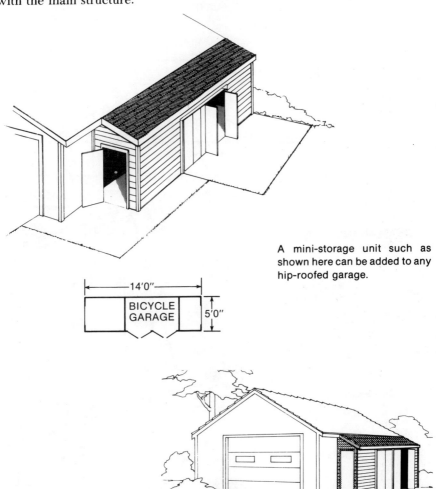

A mini-storage unit such as shown here can be added to any hip-roofed garage.

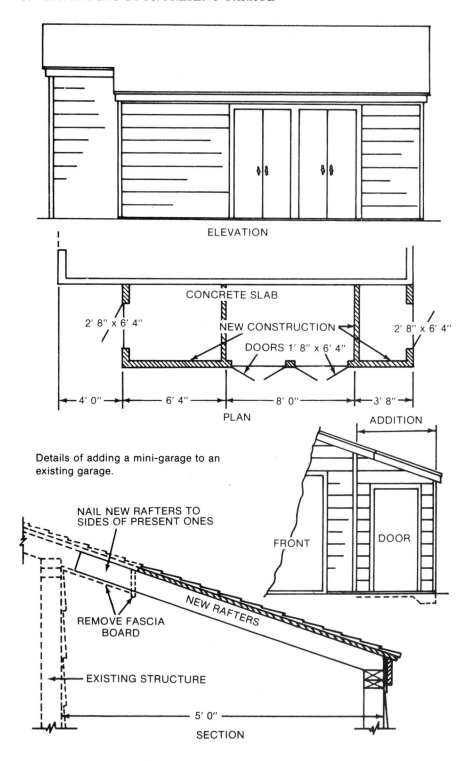

ELEVATION

CONCRETE SLAB

2′ 8″ x 6′ 4″

NEW CONSTRUCTION

DOORS 1′ 8″ x 6′ 4″

2′ 8″ x 6′ 4″

|← 4′ 0″ →| |← 6′ 4″ →| |← 8′ 0″ →| |← 3′ 8″ →|

PLAN

ADDITION

Details of adding a mini-garage to an
existing garage.

NAIL NEW RAFTERS TO
SIDES OF PRESENT ONES

FRONT

DOOR

NEW RAFTERS

REMOVE FASCIA
BOARD

EXISTING STRUCTURE

|← 5′ 0″ →|

SECTION

BOAT STORAGE. It can be a problem to find a place ashore for boat storage. All too often, if you're a boating enthusiast, the boat goes into the garage and the family car is left out in the cold. There are, fortunately, several ways to solve the problem.

Boatshed. A boatshed can be built as a free-standing shelter or as an addition to an existing garage in much the same manner as a carport. Upon selecting the site, carefully level and stake out the perimeter. Excavate for the footings and foundation; then pour the concrete, following standard practices. A slab floor could be incorporated or crushed rock could suffice. Consideration should be given to water and electrical service (by code, of course), if desired.

The framing consists of 4-by-4-inch posts on 2-by-4-inch sills, with 2-by-8-inch beams at the outside top for both wall units. Two-by-six-inch rafters are supported by the beams. Apply 1/2-inch exterior plywood diaphragms at the post/rafter joints. The wall paneling is 1/2-inch exterior plywood applied to the inside of the 4-by-4 posts. Rafter spacing may demand some trimming of the plywood sheathing for the roof. Cover the sheathing with the building paper and roofing of your choice. Also, the wood surfaces may be finished as desired.

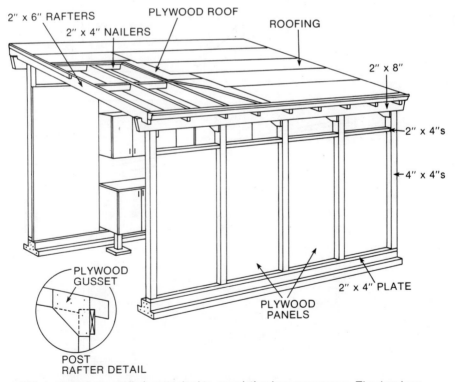

This boatshed can easily be attached to an existing house or garage. The drawings here and on pages 52 and 53 illustrate a 16-foot boatshed. You can easily add "sections" to make a 20- or 24-foot unit.

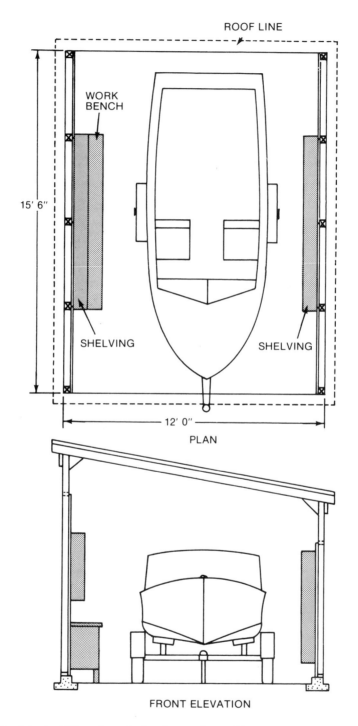

ROOF LINE

WORK
BENCH

15' 6"

SHELVING

SHELVING

12' 0"

PLAN

FRONT ELEVATION

The boatshed addition gives plenty of space for working on a boat.

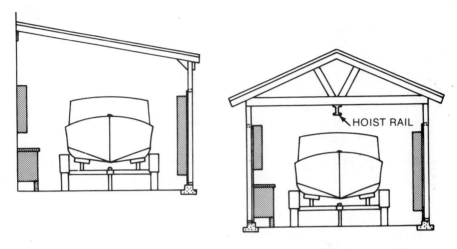

HOIST RAIL

The boatshed can be built with either a shed or hip type of roof. If a boat hoist is to be employed, be sure to use roof trusses (see page 78) to provide the necessary support for the boat or for the engine. If you have a concrete driveway (left), then you may wish to add a lean-to complete with a workbench and storage areas. Or, you may wish to have an open-air garage (right). Construct the unit, using a truss support. Great for pulling and cleaning or repairing an engine.

Boat annex to the garage. With this addition, you can back your boat right into a tandem garage annex and still have room for your car. The boat will have weather protection, work can be done on it under shelter, and there is room for motors and other extras. The swept-wing roof gives the addition a nautical air. Windows admit daylight, and a side door affords access to the boat without going through the garage.

The extension shelter is added to the back of your free-standing garage in the same fashion as when adding a garage to a house (see Chapter 3). Start the job by removing the studs and siding from the back of the garage. Pour a 17-foot (or longer) concrete slab extension of the garage floor, with suitable footings. Cut back the roof gable so that you can bolt 4-by-4-inch posts to the corners, and set similar posts on 4-foot centers for the three walls, adding horizontal nailers if you intend to use vertical siding. Fixed glass panes may be set into a few of the spaces between the horizontal frame members at the sides and back, if desired.

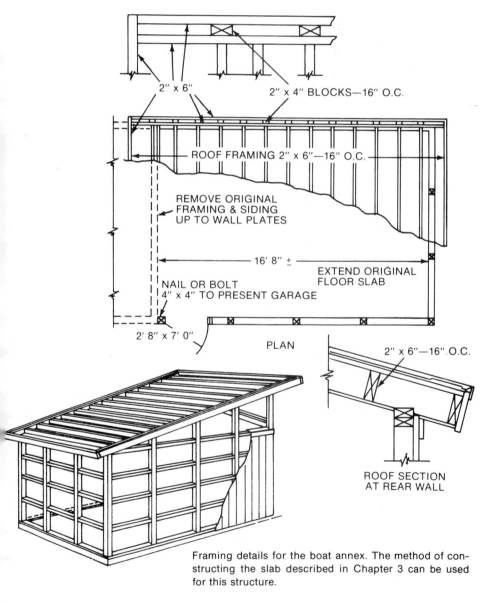

Framing details for the boat annex. The method of constructing the slab described in Chapter 3 can be used for this structure.

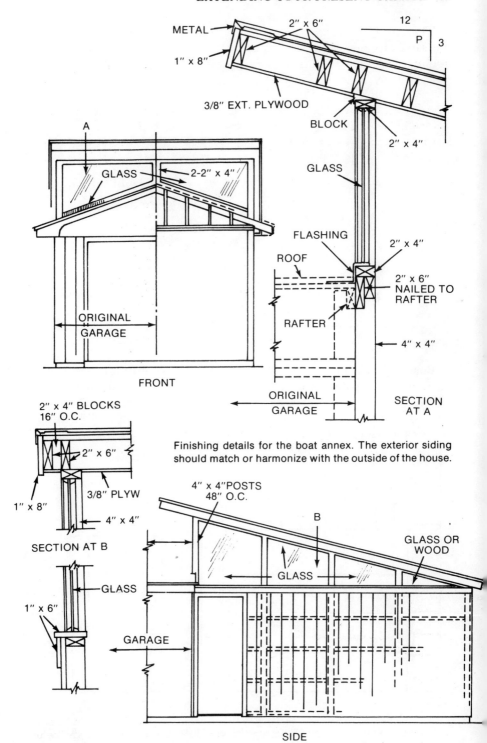

Finishing details for the boat annex. The exterior siding should match or harmonize with the outside of the house.

METAL

2" x 6"

12
P 3

1" x 8"

3/8" EXT. PLYWOOD

BLOCK

2" x 4"

A

GLASS

2-2" x 4"

GLASS

FLASHING

2" x 4"

ROOF

2" x 6" NAILED TO RAFTER

RAFTER

ORIGINAL GARAGE

4" x 4"

FRONT

ORIGINAL GARAGE

SECTION AT A

2" x 4" BLOCKS 16" O.C.

2" x 6"

3/8" PLYW

1" x 8"

4" x 4"

SECTION AT B

GLASS

1" x 6"

GARAGE

4" x 4" POSTS 48" O.C.

B

GLASS OR WOOD

GLASS

GARAGE

SIDE

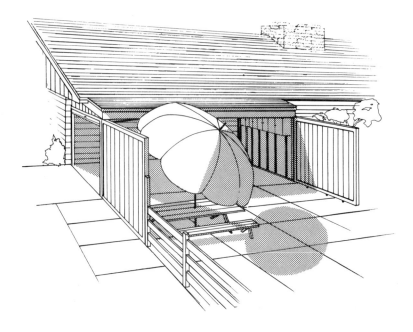

Boat shelter with patio wings. A place to keep your boat under cover the year around, a patio for outdoor living, and a place for rainy-day repairs— all are combined in a structure that economically makes use of one wall of your garage. Its outer wall consists of two hinged panels that roll on casters to screen the patio area when you want extra privacy.

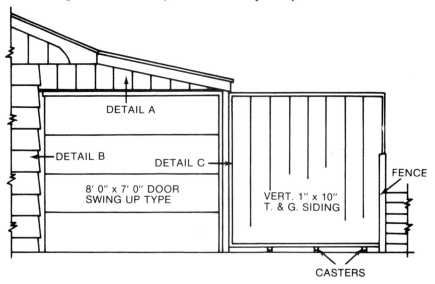

Front view of the boat shelter with patio wings. It may be attached to either a single-car garage or a double-car garage.

To begin the project, excavate for a slab foundation and set in treated 2-by-4s to create an interesting pattern of squares and allow for expansion. Fasten 4-by-6-inch posts to the existing building as in the plan view. Set up 6-by-6-inch posts with 2-by-6-inch plates on top and build out a roof extension. Cover it with roofing to match that on the main building.

Close the rear wall with vertical siding. Make the hinged wall sections of siding, framed with 2-by-4s, with quarter-round moldings in the corners. The hinged sections should also be covered with siding. A swing-up door may be added to the front for complete protection.

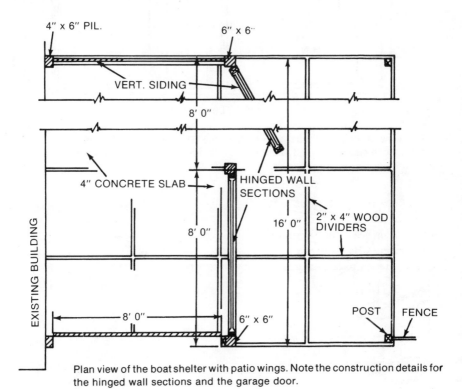

Plan view of the boat shelter with patio wings. Note the construction details for the hinged wall sections and the garage door.

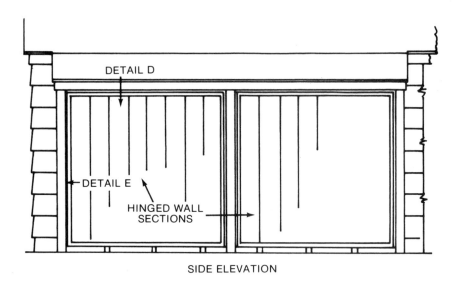

SIDE ELEVATION

Side view of the boat shelter with patio wings. The outer wing which is moved on casters can easily be rolled about to provide privacy for the dining area.

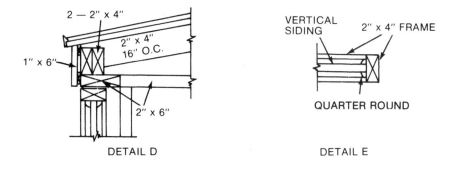

5 | Converting Your Garage Into Living Space

YOU CAN'T build up or out, but you wish to provide more living space with a minimum of structural work. What can you do? It may be possible that your attached garage can provide the solution. Actually, there are several advantages for such a conversion. First and most important is the saving that is realized because the foundation, walls, and roof are already in existence. This can amount to up to a 50 percent saving in cost where a room would otherwise have to be added by attaching a new extension to the exterior of the house. Since the garage will already have a substantial header, the closing in will consist mostly of laying a sole plate and then erecting studs. Window openings, if any, will not require individual headers.

Another point in its favor is that the room is protected from the elements, and therefore work can be done at your leisure in all kinds of weather. The work can also proceed with the least amount of inconvenience to your family.

Garage space is easily converted into an entertainment room such as that shown below.

PLANNING GARAGE CONVERSION. The converted room can be utilized as a den, bedroom, family room, or even kitchen if desired. Because a powder room is easily installed, your garage can become an attractive studio apartment. But preliminary planning is most important in converting a garage into a living space. Take time to orient the new room to the rest of the house and the outdoors so it will best serve its intended purpose. Ask the following questions:

1. How can the extra space fit into what will actually be a larger house than you now have?

2. Where should the room be entered? Should it be a dead end in the house traffic pattern, or will the room's function be such that through traffic will not disturb activities within the room?

3. Are present windows adequate, or should they be enlarged to provide a better view window and to admit more light?

4. Should the garage door be replaced with a bank of windows, view window, floor-to-ceiling glass, or sliding doors?

5. Should there be an outside entrance?

6. Where will you need electrical outlets for reading, TV, projector, etc.?

7. How many and what kind of built-in storage units do you want?

DOING THE JOB. When filling in the garage door space, it's a good idea to plan to have a picture window area or a window and door combination since much work is already done because of the header spanning the existing opening. Rough framing consists of a 2-by-4 inch sill or sole plate (a sill rests directly on the foundation; a sole plate on the floor or subfloor), cripple studs, window sill, and furring. If the header is too high, as with an 8-foot high garage door, either fur down from it or install a false header below it. Install all new windows and doors.

Possible window and door arrangements that can be built into the space formerly occupied by the overhead door.

 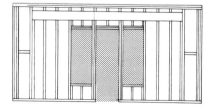

When all the openings in your former garage space have been relocated and rough-framed where you want them in the new room or rooms, you must add to heating and wiring and locate plumbing and fixtures (if a bathroom is in your conversion plans). Insulate the walls and ceiling. Fit the insulation blankets snug between the sleepers, stapling the side flanges to the wood members. When the ends of two batts are joined, make sure that they are tightly butted. Place the insulation with the vapor side up, facing the inside of the room, so that vapor does not penetrate and become trapped within the insulation material. Narrow spaces along walls, or between two sleepers that have to be placed closely together, should be packed with vermiculite granules poured into the opening and spread evenly.

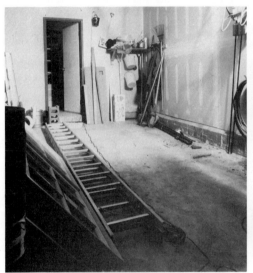 

The steps involved in converting a cluttered garage into a useful family room.

Floor finishing. If the slab is sound and cleanable, you can lay a floor directly on the concrete by using vinyl tiles or wood block flooring that is made specifically for such an application. If the floor has any large grease stains from the car crankcase, these should be thoroughly cleaned to remove a source of unpleasant odor that would penetrate the completed room. Scrub the floor with a strong detergent, preferably the kind used by service stations to clean pavements.

Wood squares can be applied with adhesive directly to the concrete surface. After adhesive is spread with a trowel, follow the manufacturer's instructions for laying the squares.

Laying self-adhesive tiles is a simple job. Just peel off the protective paper on the back of the tile and press into place directly on the concrete.

If there is a floor drain in the garage, seal it off with a cap before applying the finished floor to prevent sewer gas from rising after water in the trap has evaporated. If the drain doesn't have a threaded nipple for the cap, consult your plumber for the best way to close the drain. One method that is commonly used is to plug the nipple with okum or cement mortar, over which melted lead is poured to seal the opening.

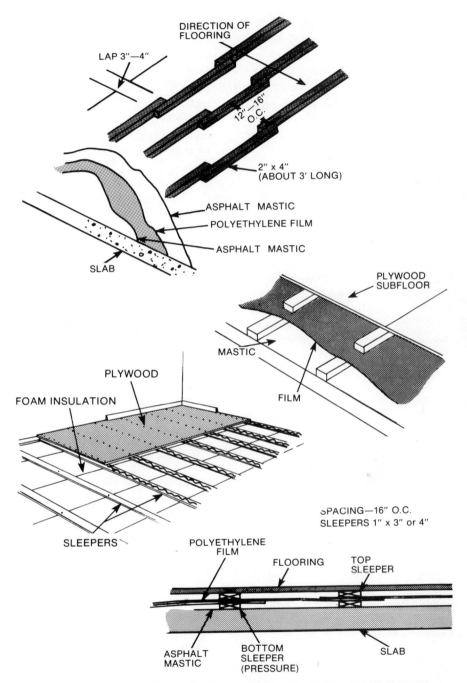

DIRECTION OF FLOORING

LAP 3"—4"

12"—16" O.C.

2" x 4" (ABOUT 3' LONG)

ASPHALT MASTIC

POLYETHYLENE FILM

ASPHALT MASTIC

SLAB

PLYWOOD SUBFLOOR

MASTIC

PLYWOOD

FOAM INSULATION

FILM

SPACING—16" O.C.
SLEEPERS 1" x 3" or 4"

SLEEPERS

POLYETHYLENE FILM

FLOORING

TOP SLEEPER

ASPHALT MASTIC

BOTTOM SLEEPER (PRESSURE)

SLAB

Where dampness is a problem or the floor is uneven, sleepers should be installed. To keep dampness under control, apply a coat of asphalt mastic and use a sheet of 4 mil polyethylene film under the plywood subfloor. Foam insulation can be placed between the sleepers to reduce heat loss through the concrete slab.

If the slab requires waterproofing or if you wish to have a more conventional type floor, there are several methods of applying a finished floor. For example, where an insulated concrete floor is desired, it is possible to install foam insulation board under a plywood wearing surface. Before applying the insulation board, be sure the floor surface you will be bonding to is structurally sound, clean and dry, and is free of oil and loose paint. Any cracks should be filled with patching cement several days prior to installation. Much heat is lost due to cold air blowing in through cracks, so take this opportunity to caulk cracks where the floor and walls meet; concrete binder works fine for this purpose.

Determine which direction the plywood should run and plan to run the furring strips at right angles to the plywood. The foam insulation board can run whichever direction is easiest for you. To install the subfloor, proceed as follows:

1. Cut the foam insulation board to fit the length.

2. Apply foam and panel adhesive in ribbons according to the instructions on the cartridge.

3. Adhere the foam insulation board to the concrete. Firmly and uniformly press the insulation board over every square foot of surface to assure an intimate bond. Repeat until all the floor surface is covered.

4. Lay the 1-by-2 furring strips on 16-inch centers over the foam insulation board, making sure that the ends of the plywood will fall along the centers of the strips. With concrete nails, fasten the furring strips every 3 feet through the foam into the concrete floor.

5. Apply a serpentine ribbon of construction adhesive over the furring strips. Lay the plywood perpendicular to the strips, and nail it to the strips with ring nails or spiral nails on 4-inch centers. The 1/2-inch plywood will provide a firm base for the finished flooring as well as adequate fire protection for the foam insulation board.

6. Sand off any irregularities at the plywood joints, and you are ready for your new carpeting. If you have chosen to install tile or sheet material and wood flooring, you will want to make the plywood joints absolutely flush by filling them with wood filler and sanding them smooth.

Finishing the walls. Inside walls and the ceiling can be done with gypsum wallboard or one of the easy-to-install 4-by-8-foot decorative plywood or hardboard wall panelings. These finishing materials may be applied with either nails, or preferably, adhesives. These adhesives, frequently called panel and plywood adhesives or mastics, can be used to bond panels, drywall, hardboard, corkboard, bulletin boards, or chalkboards to masonry, studs, drywall, or concrete. That is, paneling of all types can be bonded tightly to studs, drywall, masonry, or furring strips with these adhesives and requires few or no nails for a smooth, one-step installation. This eliminates nail pops and patching. It also eliminates the danger of marring prefinished panels with hammer marks. The adhesives also overcome structural deficiencies, fill gaps, and bridge minor framing defects. Usually dispensed from cartridges, most panel adhesives will not drip from beams or sag from vertical surfaces. The following are the basic techniques for the use of panel adhesives:

1. Remove dust and other foreign matter from the surfaces to be bonded.

2. Apply the panel adhesive to the studs only. Use a 1/8 to 1/4-inch bead where the surface will conform closely. Use a 3/8-inch or thicker bead on uneven surfaces where bridging is required.

3. After the adhesive has been applied to the studs, position the panels within 20 to 30 minutes.

4. Press the panels firmly against the studs to insure a good bond. Press only once. The adhesive will bridge the gaps automatically. Use nails or other fasteners on areas where surfaces tend to separate. Remove the fasteners after 24 hours.

5. Nail the paneling at the top and bottom with finishing nails. Finish the paneling by applying the proper moldings.

When installing paneling, the adhesive can be applied directly to the studs or furring strips. The panels are then positioned against the wall and pressed into place. Tap them into place to make sure they adhere to studs. Place nails at top and bottom to hold panels while the adhesive dries. Nails can be removed when adhesive sets.

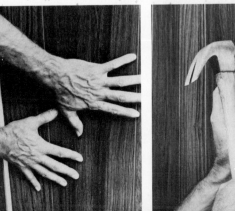

Many panel adhesives are extremely difficult to remove after they have dried. In the wet state, a suitable solvent such as mineral spirits or lighter fluid will satisfactorily remove smears or clean up tools, etc.

If the walls of your garage are of masonry block, you can build a stud wall of 2-by-3-inch lumber against the existing walls, then install insulation blankets between the studs, and attach the paneling to the studs with adhesive.

Another method of finishing masonry walls is to insulate them using plastic foam insulation (either polyurethane or polystyrene). Cement the foam boards directly to the concrete walls, then glue 1/2-inch gypsum board over the foam to provide a finished wall, as well as fire protection. But, before insulating the walls, be sure the surface to which you will be bonding is structurally sound, clean and dry, and is free of grease and loose paint. With poured concrete foundations, it is especially important that the surface is free of any form release substances that may have been used when the foundation walls were poured. Since these materials usually contain oils, greases, and/or silicones, the masonry surface should be washed down thoroughly with trisodium-phosphate (TSP) or a strong detergent.

With masonry nails or construction adhesive, attach horizontal wood strips (2 inches wide and the same thickness as the foam insulation) continuously along the top and bottom edges of the masonry walls and around windows and doors. Then, cut the foam insulation to fit around any surface projections, such as windows, wood strips, electrical outlets, and conduits. This is accomplished easily with any sharp utility knife by scoring the insulation and snapping it, or just by cutting all the way through it. Caution: Before applying any adhesive on polystyrene type foams, make certain that the adhesive is formulated for this purpose. Polystyrene foams can be severely damaged by certain solvents contained in adhesive formulations.

Following the instructions on the cartridge, apply a continuous bead of foam adhesive around the perimeter and strips in the center of the foam. Or, apply daubs the size of a golf ball on 12-inch centers around the perimeter and through the field of the foam board. Do one board of insulation at a time. When the adhesive has been applied, place the foam against the wall surface horizontally or vertically, whichever is more practical. Uniformly press the insulation board to the wall surface over every square foot to assure a positive and intimate bond. Make any necessary adjustment. Repeat this action for every board of foam insulation. Allow the adhesive to dry 24 hours before covering the foam with any other materials. However, again make sure that the adhesive you use to install the paneling is compatible with and will not damage the foam.

When all the surfaces to be insulated have been covered with insulation, you are ready to apply gypsum board. This should be cut to fit the entire height of the wall, since it will fit over the foam and the wood strips. Cut out any openings for electrical outlets and switches as needed. Then, apply foam adhesive to the gypsum board in the same manner as you did to the insulation. Stand the board vertically and adhere it to the foam, firmly and uniformly applying pressure over each square foot of surface. Use gypsum board nails

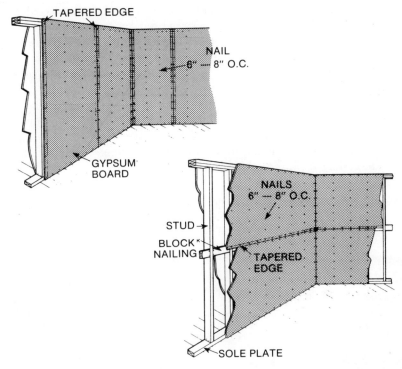

TAPERED EDGE

NAIL
6″ — 8″ O.C.

GYPSUM
BOARD

NAILS
6″ — 8″ O.C.

STUD

BLOCK
NAILING

TAPERED
EDGE

SOLE PLATE

Two methods of installing gypsum board; vertically (top) and horizontally (bottom).

at the top and bottom to fasten the panels in position until the adhesive sets.

With your room completely walled, you can now begin the final stages of the installation, which consist of taping and cementing joints and smoothing over any possible surface irregularities. (If you used adhesive to hold the panels, there are no nail holes to fill.) Joint cement, "spackle," is used to apply the tape over the tapered edge joints and to smooth and level the surface. It comes in powder form and is mixed with water to a soft putty consistency so that it can be easily spread with a trowel or putty knife. It can also be obtained in premixed form. The general procedure for taping is as follows:

1. Use a wide (5-inch) spackling knife and spread the cement in the tapered edges, starting at the top of the wall.

2. Press the tape into the recess with the putty knife until the joint cement is forced through the perforations.

3. Cover the tape with additional cement, feathering the outer edges.

4. Allow the cement to dry, sand the joint lightly, and then apply the second coat, feathering the edges. A steel trowel is sometimes used in applying the second coat. For best results, a third coat may be applied, feathering beyond the second coat.

5. After the joint cement is dry, sand smooth the area. (An electric hand vibrating sander works well.)

Interior corners between walls and ceilings may also be concealed with some type of molding. When moldings are used, taping this joint is not necessary. Wallboard corner beads at exterior corners will prevent damage to the gypsum board. They are fastened in place and covered with the joint cement. The gypsum wallboard, unless of the decorative type, is either painted or wallpapered.

While plywood, hardboard, and gypsum panels can be used on the ceiling, acoustical tile is the most popular and easiest to install of all the finished garage ceiling materials. The prefinished tile can be installed with staples or adhesive or can be held in a grid to form a drop ceiling. The latter makes an excellent ceiling for a recreation room.

Method of installing a drop-grid ceiling. After determining the height of the ceiling, a molding is nailed around the perimeter of the room. Hanger wires are attached to joists at 4-foot intervals. A string is run from molding to determine the height of main and cross ties. Once they are installed, the ceiling panels can be put in place.

(Top left) Freestanding fireplace or (top right) built-in corner fireplace will help heat garage room. (Bottom) Framing details for built-in prefabricated corner fireplace. Closely follow the specifications of the manufacturer for safe placement of fireplace or stove.

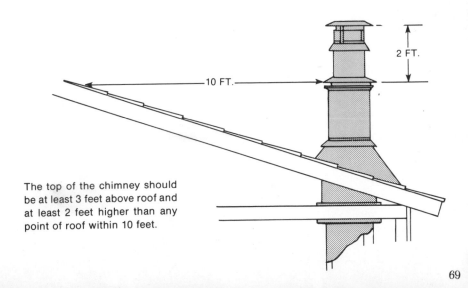

2 FT.

10 FT.

The top of the chimney should be at least 3 feet above roof and at least 2 feet higher than any point of roof within 10 feet.

Exterior finish. Before finishing the exterior of your new addition, break up and remove the concrete apron or sloped slab at the garage door. (Be sure to wear eye protection when doing this.) Use a cold chisel and heavy hammer to score the concrete in sections small enough to lift and cart away. Break the slab at score marks with a heavier sledge. The job is made easier if you dig under the slab. The exterior of the converted garage should be finished to match the house.

It's not always necessary to evict the car from the garage to get more living space. As shown above, the old garage space was made into living area, but a new garage was attached to the old one. For details on how this can be accomplished, see page 43.

6 | Building A Detached Garage

IN RECENT years, there has been a tendency toward having a garage separate from the house—and there are plenty of good reasons. A separate garage, because of its flexibility and its location on your property, can be used to fulfill many more functions than a structure attached to a house. Many of these will come to light as you study the garage designs given in this chapter. But before you start the actual building of a detached garage, here are three points to keep in mind:

1. **Check your local building requirements.** Check with your local building official to find out about any special code regulations or restrictions in your area. Sometimes there are height limits or property line set back restrictions to be considered. Also, make sure an additional separate building is allowed. And check your property lines. Precautions like these may save you a costly rebuilding job later.

2. **Match the style to your home.** Your garage should ideally be of the same architectural style as your home. But if your home isn't a definite type of architecture, select a garage design that suits your own taste. Also, while it is usually best, wherever possible, to pick finish roof and siding materials similar to those on your house, this isn't a hard and fast rule. Frequently, it's possible to select materials that will complement your home. For instance, a brick colonial house with white trim can very well be complemented by a white frame garage.

3. **Make sure the garage is big enough.** List the ways you'll be using your garage (remember you may be using it as a patio or a sheltered play area for the children), then see where it will be most convenient. Also plan for your storage needs—power mower, sports equipment, barbecue supplies, garden tools, etc. It is important to think of your future needs. You may want to add a breezeway, patio, or flower bed later. Additional inside space is handy for workbenches, cabinets, or closets.

4. **Plan the best location on your property.** Careful planning will be necessary so that the driveway will be wide and straight enough to permit easy entrance to and exit from the garage. (Details on driveway layout can be found in Chapter 10.) The garage site should be as level as possible and located where you can build the structure with a minimum amount of disturbance.

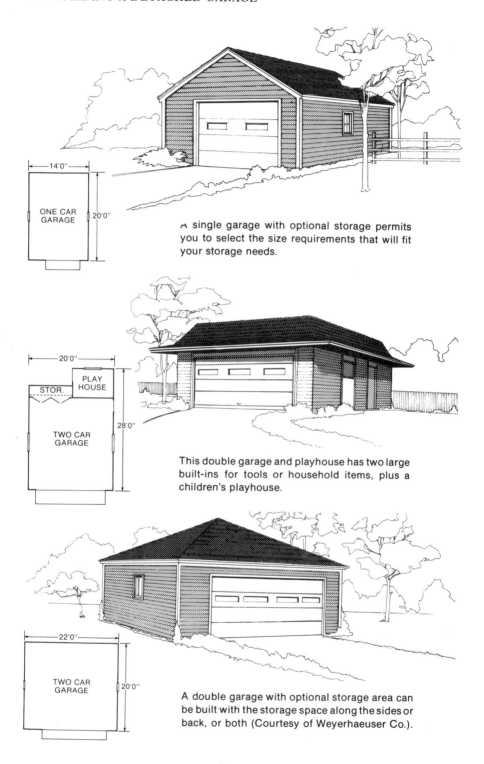

ONE CAR GARAGE — 14'0" × 20'0"

A single garage with optional storage permits you to select the size requirements that will fit your storage needs.

STOR. — PLAY HOUSE — 20'0"

TWO CAR GARAGE — 28'0"

This double garage and playhouse has two large built-ins for tools or household items, plus a children's playhouse.

TWO CAR GARAGE — 22'0" × 20'0"

A double garage with optional storage area can be built with the storage space along the sides or back, or both (Courtesy of Weyerhaeuser Co.).

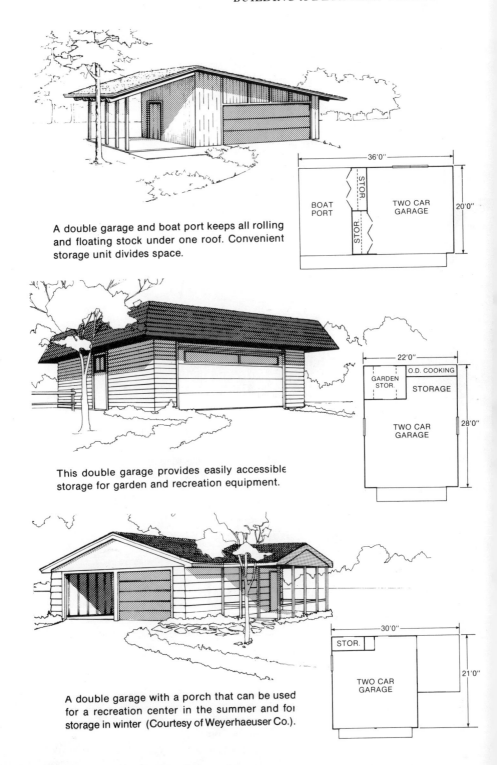

A double garage and boat port keeps all rolling and floating stock under one roof. Convenient storage unit divides space.

This double garage provides easily accessible storage for garden and recreation equipment.

A double garage with a porch that can be used for a recreation center in the summer and for storage in winter (Courtesy of Weyerhaeuser Co.).

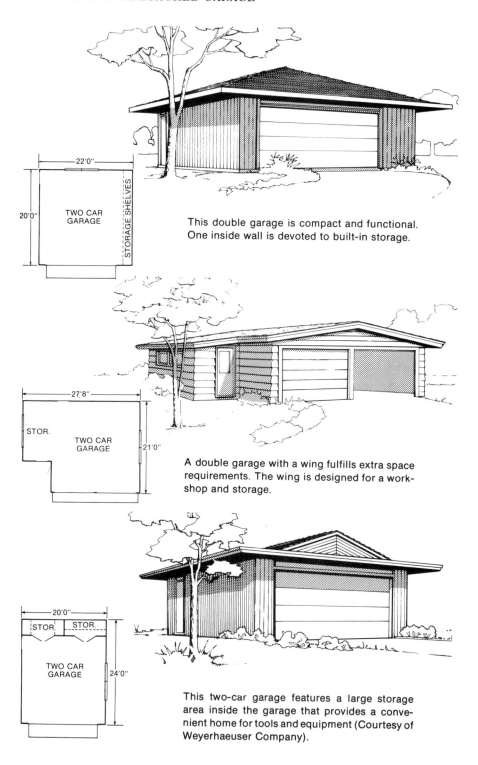

22'0"

20'0"   TWO CAR
        GARAGE   STORAGE SHELVES

This double garage is compact and functional.
One inside wall is devoted to built-in storage.

27'8"

STOR.
        TWO CAR
        GARAGE   21'0"

A double garage with a wing fulfills extra space
requirements. The wing is designed for a workshop and storage.

20'0"

STOR.   STOR.

TWO CAR
GARAGE   24'0"

This two-car garage features a large storage
area inside the garage that provides a convenient home for tools and equipment (Courtesy of
Weyerhaeuser Company).

WOOD FRAMED DETACHED GARAGE. Separate garages of wood frame construction are the most popular types and are well within the building abilities of the average do-it-yourselfer. Although twelve garage designs and their floor plans are given in this chapter, we'll show here the construction details of the gabled-roof two-car garage. The construction details of the other wood framed garages are basically the same.

Laying out the concrete floor. Once the location of the garage on the property has been decided, the first job is to lay out the ground for the concrete floor and foundation wall. The next step, after the corners of the garage have been established, is to determine the lines and grades as aids in keeping the work level and true. The batter board is one of the methods used to locate and retain the outline of a detached garage. The height of the boards is sometimes established to conform to the height of the slab.

Small stakes are first located accurately at each corner of the garage area with nails driven in their tops to indicate the outside line of the slab. To assure square corners, measure the diagonals to see if they are the same length. The corners can also be squared by measuring along one side a distance of 3 feet

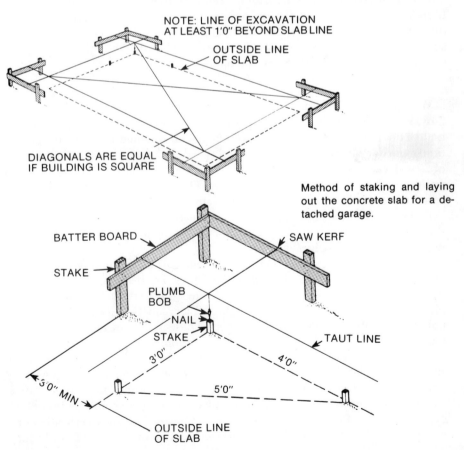

Method of staking and laying out the concrete slab for a detached garage.

and along the adjoining side 4 feet. The diagonals will then measure 5 feet, if the corner is square. Once the corners have been located, batter boards can be installed as described on page 34 and the earth removed from the area to be occupied by the floor and foundation walls.

The foundation wall should extend above the finished grade around the outside of the garage by about 6 inches so that the wood finish and framing members will be adequately protected from soil moisture and will be well above the grass line. The slab perimeter should extend a minimum of 1 foot below the ground level (grade). In colder parts of our country, it may be necessary to extend the foundation wall to 3 or more feet below grade. The building code in force in your locality should give you information on how deep the slab wall should be. In some cases, it may be necessary to pour a foundation wall or footing first. Then, add the concrete garage floor at a later date. But, in any case, the slab or floor proper consists of 4-inch concrete poured on a 5-inch bed of evenly spread gravel. The gravel ensures a firm base and proper drainage under the garage. To guarantee a strong, durable garage floor, it's a good idea to lay 3/8-inch tie rods or wire mesh in the concrete.

As described in Chapter 3, forms are required to hold the poured concrete foundation until it sets. (The proper method of pouring concrete is fully described on page 36.) Anchor bolts or clips are placed in concrete while it's still plastic to hold the base plate. Be sure to anchor the base plate in places where the studs or corners won't be nailed.

Wall framing. To frame the walls, first build the bottom plate by laying 2-by-4s on their face around the sides and back of the floor. If you plan to build a door in one side wall, leave a 35-inch wide opening at the correct position in the bottom plate for the door and two door jambs. Also cut two pieces of 2-by-4, each 18-1/2 inches long, and lay these at the front of the floor, butting against the 2-by-4 bottom plate at the sides. The entire base or sole plate is fastened down to the concrete floor by means of the anchor clips.

Each wall frame section can be built and raised into place separately, or the studs and plates may be fastened together individually. The method you use will depend on the help available.

The wall studs are placed 16 inches on center. If local building codes permit, the studs may be placed 24 inches on center. To speed the erection of the walls, framing clips can be used to fasten the studs to the sole plate and flat plate ties to hold the top plate to the studs. Flat plate ties can also be used to hold the top plates together at the corners. These metal ties and clips are fastened with barbed nails rather than the common type.

The overhead garage door frame usually requires two 2-by-4-inch jambs and a 1-1/8-inch finished board on each side. A rough opening width plus the thickness of the finish frame board should equal the width of the garage door. A 2-inch thick and at least 4-inch wide piece of lumber should be fastened behind the 2-by-4 jamb to hold the track and hardware. The overhead door header should be a double 2-by-8 for 8-foot doors, or a double 2-by-12 for

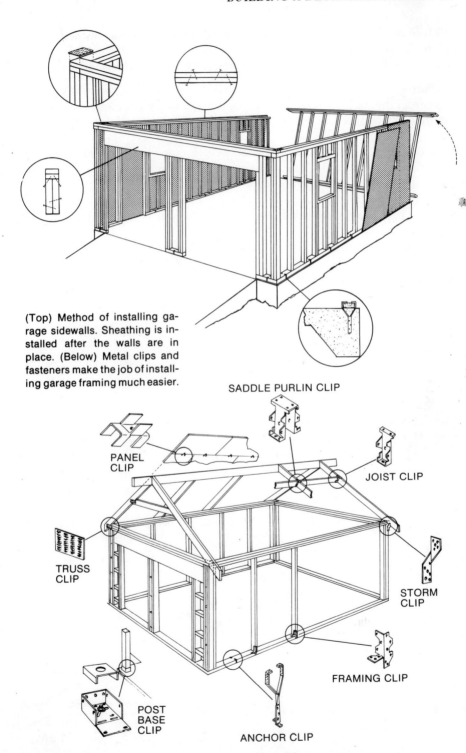

(Top) Method of installing garage sidewalls. Sheathing is installed after the walls are in place. (Below) Metal clips and fasteners make the job of installing garage framing much easier.

SADDLE PURLIN CLIP

PANEL CLIP

JOIST CLIP

TRUSS CLIP

STORM CLIP

FRAMING CLIP

POST BASE CLIP

ANCHOR CLIP

15-foot or wider doors. A 1-1/8-inch board is fastened to the header to complete the overhead door frame. Carefully check the size of the overhead door and allow for proper fitting of the track in relation to the door.

Putting on the roof. With the side wall frames in place, the next step is to construct the roof framing. This can be done in a conventional manner as described in Chapter 3, or by using roof trusses. The latter offers several advantages:

• Better space **utilization.** No posts or columns obstruct garage areas.

• Easier **construction.** The roof trusses can be built on the floor and raised into place. This reduces climbing and scaffold work.

• Greater **strength.** Properly designed and constructed trusses carry a greater roof load while using less material than the conventional rafter and joist system.

The illustration here can serve as a guide when measuring roof trusses. The truss length (A) is the length of the bottom chord (B). Truss length for frame construction is the distance between the outside face of the top plates (C).

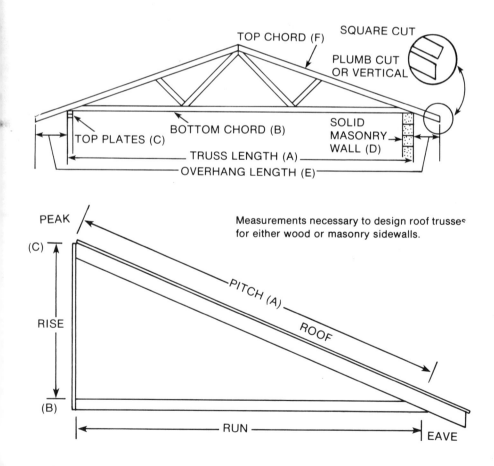

Measurements necessary to design roof trusses for either wood or masonry sidewalls.

With solid masonry construction, the truss length is the distance between the outside face of the masonry wall (D) or outside face of the bearing plates. The overhang length (E) is the horizontal distance from the end of the bottom chord (B) to the bottom edge of the rafter or top chord (F). The spacing of the trusses in most construction is 24 inches on center, instead of the usual 16 inches on center used in conventional framing. The 24-inch spacing fulfills the FHA, VA, and conventional standards. The roof pitch is the rise of the rafter (top chord) in relation to 1/2 of the truss length. Pitch (A) refers to the angle or slope of the rafters. This angle or slope can be referred to in inches of vertical rise (B to C) to a horizontal foot. For instance, a 7/12 roof will rise 7 inches for each horizontal foot it runs.

After accurately cutting all the roof members to the proper lengths and angles, the simplest and most economical way to assemble trusses is to use a jig. To do this, proceed as follows:

1. Lay out, cut, and assemble one complete truss. Securely fasten all joints with the proper size truss clips.

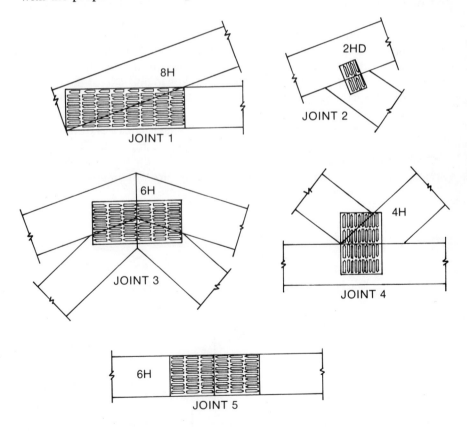

Various sizes of truss clips and how they are installed for the different truss joints.

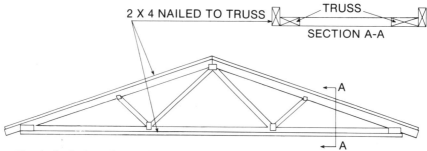

SECTION A-A

Simple jig that can be used to make duplicate roof trusses.

2. Nail on 2-by-4 lumber pieces on edge around the perimeter of the completed truss to form a jig. Place this jig on a floor, sawhorses, or other solid surface.

3. Assemble the remainder of the trusses in the jig. Once all but one of the necessary number of trusses are made, remove the 2-by-4 lumber pieces from the perimeter of the jig and use it as the final truss for the job.

When fastening with truss clips, it is best to use a regular 20-ounce carpenter's hammer, hitting three nails at a time. The nails should be driven down flush with the adjoining steel. Do not attempt to drive the nails all the way through the slots. After applying truss clips to one side of the truss, remove the truss from the jig, turn it over onto a flat surface or place it between sawhorses, and apply clips to the other side.

When installing roof trusses, it is advisable to have at least one other person to assist you. Then, proceed as follows, taking each step in the proper order:

1. After the walls are erected, lift the trusses onto the top plates of the two side walls, placing them so that the truss peaks are pointing downward.

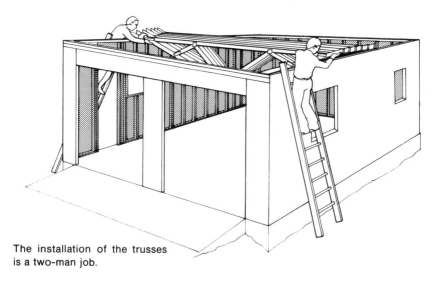

The installation of the trusses is a two-man job.

2. Place two stepladders against the outside walls of the building. Move the first truss into place at the end of the building and swing it into an upright position with a pole or two men working together. Reasonable care should be exercised to prevent racking in the turning-over process.

3. Be sure it is centered; then temporarily toenail the truss into place. Do the same at the opposite side of the building.

4. Nail a chalk line into position from one truss peak to the other. Draw it tightly into a straight line.

5. Tip up one truss at a time. The peak should be exactly under the taut line. Measure between the trusses along the top plate to be sure they are exactly the required 24 inches apart. Measure from center-to-center of each truss.

6. Fasten each truss to the top plate with a framing clip, using one on each end. Use 1-7/16-inch barbed nails to hold the framing clips. After erecting the end truss, temporarily brace it before setting up the other trusses. All of the trusses should be braced laterally to prevent them from toppling over.

Once all the trusses are in place, the 1/2-inch 4-by-8 foot plywood sheathing or equivalent can be installed. Connect the panels with typical panel clips, then nail them down to the rafters. Cover the plywood with 15-pound asphalt roll roofing material. When applying asphalt strip shingles, it is important to apply a double layer of shingles at the bottom row on each side of the roof, with the top edge of the bottom layer turned downward. Stagger the next

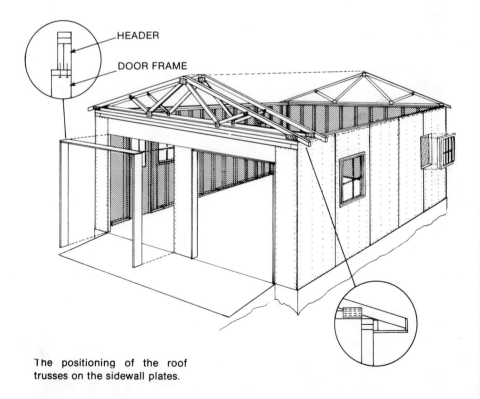

The positioning of the roof trusses on the sidewall plates.

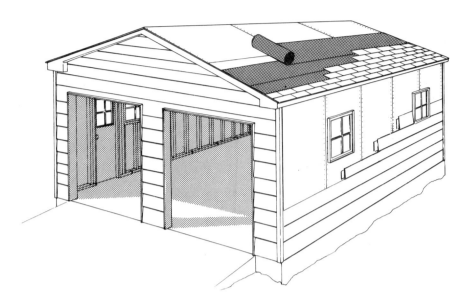

Finishing touches are added to the garage, including siding and the roof—which consists of roofing felt and shingles.

course so that neither slots nor edges fall over the slots or edges of the lower course. A metal strip is applied over the ridge after the shingle application is completed. The next step is to finish off the eaves, according to your plan or blueprint.

Completing the job. After all of the windows and doors—other than the overhead one—are put in, sheathing—either wood or nonwood—should be installed on the walls. The sides may then be finished with shingles or other desired siding material.

Wood shingles and shakes may be used over wood or plywood sheathing. If sheathing is 3/8-inch plywood, use threaded nails. For nonwood sheathing, 1-by-3- or 1-by-4-inch wood nailing strips are used as a base. In the most common installation method, one course is simply laid over the other. The shin-

The completed garage. Various siding materials may be applied to match those on the house and other buildings on your property.

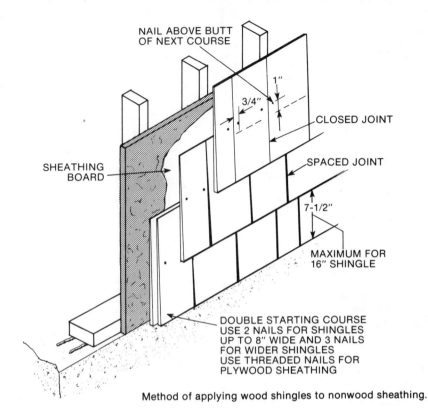

NAIL ABOVE BUTT
OF NEXT COURSE

1"

3/4"

CLOSED JOINT

SHEATHING
BOARD

SPACED JOINT

7-1/2"

MAXIMUM FOR
16" SHINGLE

DOUBLE STARTING COURSE
USE 2 NAILS FOR SHINGLES
UP TO 8" WIDE AND 3 NAILS
FOR WIDER SHINGLES
USE THREADED NAILS FOR
PLYWOOD SHEATHING

Method of applying wood shingles to nonwood sheathing.

gles can be second-grade because only one-half or less of the butt portion is exposed. Shingles should not be soaked before application but should usually be laid up with about 1/8- to 1/4-inch space between adjacent shingles to allow for expansion during rainy weather. When a "siding effect" is desired, shingles should be laid up so that they are only lightly in contact. Prestained or treated shingles provide the best results for this system.

Bevel or lap wood siding may be installed starting with the bottom course. It is normally blocked out with a starting strip the same thickness as the top of the siding board. Each succeeding course overlaps the upper edge of the lower course. Siding should be nailed to each stud or on 16-inch centers. When plywood or wood sheathing or spaced wood nailing strips are used over nonwood sheathing, 7d or 8d nails (2-1/4 and 2-1/2 inches long) may be used for 3/4-inch thick siding. However, if gypsum or fiberboard sheathing is used, the 10d nail is recommended to penetrate into the stud. For 1/2-inch thick siding, nails may be 1/4 inch shorter than those used for 3/4-inch siding. The nails should be located far enough up from the butt to miss the top of the lower siding course. This clearance distance is usually 1/8 inch. This allows for slight movement of the siding due to moisture changes without causing splitting. Such an allowance is especially required for the wider sidings of 8- to 12-inch widths.

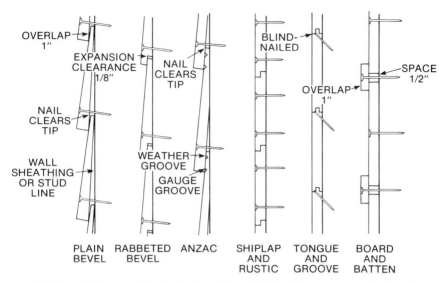

PLAIN   RABBETED   ANZAC   SHIPLAP   TONGUE   BOARD
BEVEL   BEVEL   AND   AND   AND
                               RUSTIC   GROOVE   BATTEN

Installation of the more popular horizontal wood siding. These are manufactured in
nominal 1-inch thicknesses and in widths from 4 to 12 inches. Normally, one or two
8d or 9d nails should be used at each stud crossing, depending on the width.

Drop wood siding is installed in much the same way as lap siding except for spacing and nailing. Dolly Varden, drop, and similar sidings have a constant exposure distance. This face width is normally 5-1/4 inches for 1-by-6-inch siding and 7-1/4 inches for 1-by-8-inch siding. Normally, one or two 8d or 9d nails should be used at each stud crossing, depending on the width. The length of the nail depends on the type of sheathing used, but penetration into the stud or through the wood backing should be at least 1-1/2 inches. Horizontally applied matched paneling in narrow widths should be blind-nailed at the tongue with a corrosion-resistant finishing nail. For widths greater than 6 inches, an additional nail should be used.

When installing vinyl siding, the inside and outside corner posts are installed first. Then, install a starter strip along the bottom of the garage. The first panel is placed in the starter strip and securely locked. Panels are fastened with nails that are centered in the nailing slots. Check the course to insure proper alignment with windows and eaves. Allowances should be made for expansion and contraction by leaving approximately 1/4 inch at all corner posts and channels. If individual corner caps are used, cut back the panels 1/4 inch from the corner. Vinyl panel ends should be lapped approximately one-half of the factory-prenotched end. Succeeding courses are similarly installed. Stagger the end laps so that one is not directly above the other, unless separated by three courses. Check every fifth or sixth course for alignment. Do not force the panels up or down when nailing in position. A panel should not be under vertical tension or compression when it is nailed. Always overlap the joints away from entrances and from the point of greatest traffic. This will improve the overall appearance of the installation.

Aluminum and steel siding are installed in much the same manner as vinyl. Always be sure to follow the instructions of the manufacturer to the letter.

To complete the garage, the overhead garage door must be installed in the already constructed frame. Complete details on the installation of garage doors are given in Chapter 7.

DETACHED GARAGES OF CONCRETE BLOCK. Concrete block also makes a substantial, serviceable garage. The construction of this type of garage is easy, and the walls are strong enough to support extra living or storage space above the garage portion. Most of the plans illustrated earlier in this chapter and detailed for wood framing can be adapted to concrete block construction.

Building the footer. A concrete base or "footer" must be poured to provide a foundation for the concrete block wall. On level, firm ground, no forms may be necessary. Make the footing trench twice as wide as the wall. If you're using 8-inch blocks, make the trench 16 inches wide. The footing's thickness should be slightly larger than the wall. Thus, an 8-inch wall gets a 12-inch thick footing.

After establishing the location of the footing and walls as described earlier in this chapter, drive the stakes around the perimeter and connect them with a string line. With a spirit level and board, level these stakes. Digging can now begin. The line and stakes provide a guide for uniform depth. For load-bearing or free-standing walls higher than 4 feet, footers should be poured below the frost line. The U.S. Weather Bureau can provide this information. It is also recommended that local building codes be checked. Where soil is especially compact or clay-like, and in areas with cold winter temperatures, a 4-inch base of sand and/or gravel is recommended.

Detached concrete block garages can be very attractive.

After completion of the trench, drive the wood stakes in the trench at 3-foot intervals to the level of the line. These will indicate the top of the concrete footer to be poured. A level and board should again be used. Using a 1:2-1/4:3 mix or a proper ready-mixed concrete, fill the trench level to the top of the stakes. Jab a shovel blade into the freshly poured concrete at frequent intervals to make sure that all of the air pockets are removed. Allow the footer to set at least overnight before laying the wall.

Laying the block. Drive a stake at each end of wall position, and stretch a line to indicate the side and top of the first course (layer) of blocks. The stake should be as tall as the top of the wall, so that the line can be raised and leveled again in the same plane as each course is completed. The first course (layer) of blocks should first be positioned without mortar to check the fit, allowing for a 3/8-inch joint between the blocks. To help align the blocks accurately, a chalk line should be used to mark the footing.

Mix the mortar following the directions on the bag. Spread a 1-inch thick coat of mortar on top of the footer the length of three or four blocks. Position an end or corner block first, tapping it into place with the trowel handle. Spread the mortar ("butter") on one end of the next block, and position. As each block is squeezed into position, leave a 3/8-inch mortar joint. Each block should be checked with a level for both vertical and horizontal trueness. Following the laying of every three or four courses, use a jointer tool to remove excess mortar and compress the joints. Use a coarse cloth to remove mortar from the face of the blocks. After completion of the first course, position both the corner blocks for the second course, and move the line to the top of the blocks.

When additional vertical strength in the wall is necessary, as in building a garage into the slope of a hill, and where the wall must resist lateral force, extra reinforcement may be needed. Reinforcing bars (available at your supply store) may be inserted vertically into the footer to the height of the wall at intervals coinciding with the holes in the blocks. The holes should then be filled by pouring "dry" mortar mix into them. Then add just enough water to make the mortar pliable.

Since the garage wall is at least 20 feet in length, control joints are a must. Actually, a control joint is just a vertical joint from the top to the bottom of the wall. Stresses that accumulate in the wall relieve themselves at the control joint before a crack can form. There are a number of types of control joints built into concrete masonry walls, but the most preferred types are either the Michigan or the tongue-and-groove. The so-called Michigan type of control joint uses conventional flanged block units. A strip of building paper is curled into the end core covering the end of the block on one side of the joint and, as the block on the other side of the joint is laid, the core is filled with mortar. The filling bonds to one block, but the paper prevents bond to the block on the other side of the control joint. Thus, the control joint permits longitudinal movement of the wall while the mortar plug transmits transverse loads.

Steps in laying up concrete block walls: (Left to right—top to bottom) A full mortar bed is necessary for laying the first course. The blocks are leveled by tapping with a trowel handle. The trowel handle is also used to assure that the blocks are plumb (vertically straight). A mason's level is used as a straightedge to assure correct alignment of the block. Be sure mortar is applied uniformly on the bed joints. Light tapping will bring a block into position with the string line. The closure block is then carefully lowered into place. The corner block must be checked for levelness and plumb. After the wall is complete, tool by horizontal and vertical joints.

The special tongue-and-groove type control joint blocks are manufactured in sets consisting of full- and half-length units. The tongue of one special unit fits into the groove of another special unit or into the open end of a regular flanged stretcher. The units are laid in mortar exactly the same as any other masonry units.

Control joints should be employed roughly every 8 feet in a garage wall. The best location for a control joint is at a window or door. To make a control joint, lay up the blocks in mortar in the same manner as for other vertical joints. But before the mortar hardens, rake it out to a depth of 3/4 inch. The mortar remaining in the control joint forms a backing to confine a caulking compound or similar elastic weathertight material. First, however, to prevent absorption of oils from certain caulking compounds, the side faces of the raked joint should be primed with shellac, aluminum paint, or other sealer, but the inner face of the joint should be greased or given some other bond-breaker. Then the caulking is applied by using a caulking gun. Care must be taken not to smear the caulking onto the face of the wall.

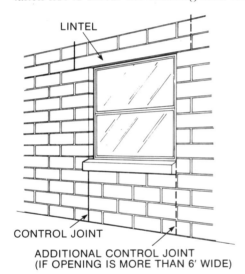

LINTEL

CONTROL JOINT

ADDITIONAL CONTROL JOINT
(IF OPENING IS MORE THAN 6′ WIDE)

(Left) Control joints are usually located at window openings to avoid random cracking.

The two most popular control joints: (below left) Michigan-type with tar paper and (below right) the tongue-and-groove unit.

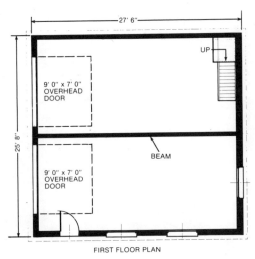

27' 6"

9' 0" x 7' 0"
OVERHEAD
DOOR

UP

25' 8"

BEAM

9' 0" x 7' 0"
OVERHEAD
DOOR

FIRST FLOOR PLAN

A large double-car concrete block garage with an apartment or workshop on the second floor. The 27-foot, 6-inch depth permits the location of the staircase at the rear of the garage without taking up any vehicle space. Complete facilities—bath and kitchen—can be added to make a good sized one-room apartment. If more daylight is needed for the second floor area, a skylight can be installed in the roof.

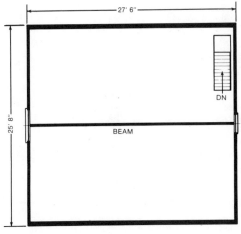

27' 6"

DN

25' 8"

BEAM

SECOND FLOOR PLAN

89

Constructing truss roof and finishing exterior of concrete block garage/apartment.

A metal or wood lintel should be put over all door and window openings to provide support at these weak points in the wall. Lay 4-inch thick blocks on them to make an 8-inch wall. This same technique can be used to support heavy floor beams.

To support the roof framing, a wood top plate must be anchored to the wall around its perimeter. To prepare for setting anchor bolts, stuff paper at a depth of 4 inches in the cores of the blocks every 4 feet of the top course. This forms a barrier preventing anchor mortar from dropping into the block cores below. Place some mortar mix in this upper part of the core with the anchor bolt centered and extending 2-1/2 inches above the top of the blocks. After the mortar mix has cured, install the 2-by-8-inch boards as a plate.

Installation of the roof. Allow the block walls to cure for 48 hours before installing the roof trusses. (See page 78 for details on how to install trusses.) Then install the roof, using plywood sheathing as roof panels. Finish with asphalt shingles. Paint all of the wood trim. The gable areas may be completed with blocks, siding, or shingles. After the garage has been closed in, the concrete floor can be poured and trowel finished. The slab thickness should be a minimum of 4 inches. Since the floor must slope toward the doorway, the subgrade under it should also be sloped for uniform floor thickness. But, the line around the edge of the wall should be level. Therefore, establish the level line first. Then, place the screeds to slope away from it. The screeds themselves can be 2-by-2-inch wood stakes driven into the subgrade. Once the concrete is placed all around them, the strike-off board is held at the level line at one end and resting on the screed at the other. After the concrete is struck-off, the screeds are removed and their space is filled in with concrete.

When pouring a large slab, it is a good idea to space control joints at 10- to 15-foot intervals (see page 149). To prevent floor cracking in a two-car garage, for example, the floor should be jointed into four separate slabs. Cut them 1/5 the depth of the floor.

Once the roof and exterior are finished, the job can be completed by pouring the concrete floor. As shown below, the floor is first struck-off and then troweled.

If desired, you can finish the concrete block walls of your garage with one of the new, colorful glass-reinforced, surface-bonding cements or stuccos. To apply any of these materials, wet the wall uniformly with water. This prevents excessive absorption of water from the stucco mix. If the surface dries prior to application, re-wet it; however, avoid saturating the blocks. It is important that all of the blocks be completely free of paint, oil, dirt, dust, or foreign materials which interfere with bonding. Mix the plastic stucco according to the directions on the package. Starting at the bottom, and with a finishing trowel in an upward sweeping motion, completely cover the wall surface with the stucco to a minimum thickness of 1/8 inch. Masonry cement paints may also be used to finish and color the concrete blocks.

PREFABRICATED GARAGES. Up to this point in the chapter, the basic concern has been with the detached garage built from "scratch." For those who wish to save time and effort, a "pre-cut" or "pre-assembled" garage may be good for you.

The pre-cut garage package, which comes with all the pieces cut to fit by the supplier, costs more to construct than a scratch-built garage, but does away with many cutting problems and time. It does, however, require the same amount of labor and technique in assembling as a scratch-built unit.

The pre-assembled package is available with all the components put together, including prebuilt trusses and wall panels. Such a package costs more, but saves you both cutting and assembling of major components. Even so, it's possible to save from 25 to 35 percent more by purchasing and putting together a pre-assembled garage than when having a contractor build one for you.

Sometimes it's possible to convert an outbuilding into a detached garage. As shown above, a small barn was made over into a two-car garage and a studio apartment.

ELECTRICITY FOR A DETACHED GARAGE. Electricity will do many things to make your detached garage more useful. The style and construction of your home will determine how the circuits are run from the service panel to the garage.

When the service is in the basement, wiring is generally brought to the outside either through the masonry wall of the basement or through the sill on top of the foundation. Factors to be considered are whether the installation is to be underground or overhead. If underground, going directly through the basement wall and coming out below ground level on the outside is the least conspicuous method of installation. Where convenient shrubbery will hide the conduit, it may be easier to come out through the sill. Either of these methods may be chosen when the wiring is to be overhead. In this case, since a length of conduit will have to run up the side of the house, it's best to come out of the basement at a point where shrubbery will partially conceal the installation. Occasionally, in frame construction, the circuit for overhead wiring can be fished up through the walls to a point of departure at the desired elevatior of the house.

Circuits run underground offer a number of advantages to the homeowner They are not subject to damage from storms or exposed to mechanical damage. Most important, such circuits are invisible and don't, therefore, mar the appearance of the grounds and gardens.

The most economical underground installation for both feeders and branch circuits is Type UF (underground feeder) cable. This cable is approved by the National Electrical Code for direct burial in the ground without additional protection.

Underground cable is laid in a trench deep enough to prevent possible damage from normal spading. The bottom of the trench should be free from stones. This is easily accomplished by using a layer of sand or sifted dirt in the bottom of the trench. Cable is laid directly on top of this layer. When cable enters the building or leaves the ground, slack should be provided in the form of an "S" curve, to permit expansion with extreme changes in temperature. Where cable enters a building, after the cable has been installed, fill all openings through the foundation with sealing compound so that water from rain or melting snow cannot follow the cable into the building.

The National Electrical Code requires that underground feeder cables must be installed in continuous lengths from outlet to outlet and from fitting to fitting. Splices can be made only within a proper enclosure.

In some areas of the yard, where it is felt that digging might accidentally occur to the depth of the cable, a 1-by-2-inch running board can be laid over the cable before the trench is filled. Under driveways or roadways, or where heavy loading might occur, it is also desirable to use a board.

For outdoor wiring in sections of the country that are known to be termite infested or subject to attack by rodents, or wherever extra protection for the Type UF underground circuits is required, galvanized rigid steel conduit or lead-sheathed armor cable may be used for mechanical protection. When rigid conduit for the complete circuit run is used, feeders and branch circuits may be of any approved type of moisture-resistant wire such as Types TW, RW, or RHW.

Where the ground consists of a great deal of rock or ledge, it will be found a great deal easier and more economical to run outdoor wiring overhead. Overhead wiring can also be used effectively for certain lighting requirements such as floodlighting and for ornamental post lighting, provided, of course, that the overhead wire can be run high enough for proper clearance. Service drop, service entrance, or weatherproof wire of approved types may be used. Rigid conduit must be used for mechanical protection wherever the wire enters or leaves the ground. Drip loops at the point where the wire leaves the building and where it is attached to the pole are also required.

The height by which overhead wiring should clear the ground is generally controlled by local ordinance. In general, points to watch are clearances over driveways and walkways; possibility of damage caused by falling branches; isolation from window locations to prevent the conductors from being touched by persons at windows; locations such as flagpoles, TV masts, weather vanes, etc., that might foul the overhead wiring in windstorms or under conditions of ice loading.

Water can be run underground to the garage in much the same way as the electric line. Use plastic pipe, but since the detached garage most likely won't be heated during the winter months, be sure to provide a shut-off valve and drain cock in the basement so that the garage line can be turned off and drained.

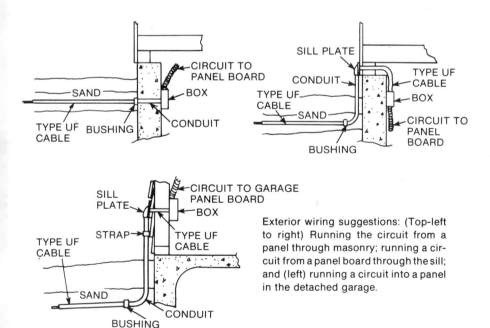

Exterior wiring suggestions: (Top-left to right) Running the circuit from a panel through masonry; running a circuit from a panel board through the sill; and (left) running a circuit into a panel in the detached garage.

7 | The Garage Door

THE SELECTION of a new or replacement garage door is most important. It must be remembered that, in the case of an attached garage, for example, the garage door may be 20 to 30 percent of your home's face. Therefore, it must be as beautiful as possible.

The "garage door decor" possibilities are nearly limitless—in both ready-made styles and creative designs of your own. For instance, you can choose from a multitude of standard quality wood panel doors to match a wide variety of architectural styles or gain a rich looking custom-crafted effect by installing any of four stock patterns of carved door. Or, perhaps your home would benefit from a smooth-surface flush panel door to which you can apply painted designs, moldings, windows, and trimwork to suit your taste. Even standard wood panel doors gain distinction with the addition of stock carved rosette plaques.

All "door decor" takes is some care in matching your architectural style with the right door. Be picky; don't leave garage door selection to after-thoughts. It's more than just the largest moving part of your home; it's also part of your home's appearance, personality, and character.

Proper garage door decor can add beauty to a house. Select the design that best fits the architectural style of your home (Courtesy of Clopay Corp. and Frantz Mfg. Co.).

GARAGE DOOR TYPES AND STYLES. Basically, there are three types of garage doors: (1) hinge or swing-out; (2) swing-up; and (3) roll-up. However, in recent years, thanks to the perfection of garage door hardware and counterbalancing equipment, the two latter types have all but replaced old-fashioned swinging doors.

Swing-up doors. Various types of counterbalancing devices are employed to offset the weight of the garage door. With the swing-up arrangement, a one-piece, rigid door is tilted or swung up and down. Either of two types of hardware are used: (1) jamb and (2) pivot. With either type, a swing-out space of about 3 to 4 feet is required.

Operating on the leverage principle, the jamb hardware is attached to the two upright wood members (the jambs) that form the sides of the garage door opening. This hardware arrangement requires an overhead track at both ends of the garage door.

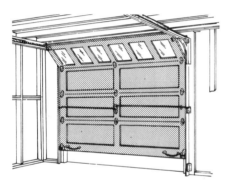
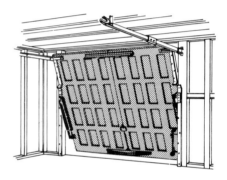

TRACK FOR ROLL-UP DOOR   TRACK FOR SWING-UP DOOR

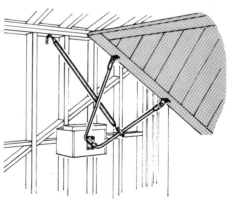

JAMB TYPE   OFFSET PIVOT

The four major types of overhead garage doors.

Pivot hardware, which requires no track of any kind, is bolted to the side of the garage building and works the door by swinging it up and down. The installation of pivot hardware is not recommended when the garage building is much wider than the door opening.

Roll-up doors. The roll-up type, which uses a three or four section door, is the most popular of all overhead types. It is available with either two extension springs—one at each side of the door—or a single torsion spring that extends across the top of the door opening. The torsion spring and its mechanism is somewhat more expensive, but generally provides a smoother and more consistent action.

The garage door hardware and counterbalancing devices should be selected to suit the door. Most jamb and pivot hardware, as well as the two extension spring roll-up type, is good for doors under 150 pounds. For doors over this weight, the torsion spring roll-up type is usually recommended.

Door materials. Overhead garage doors are available that are made of wood, fiberglass, aluminum, and steel. Each material has its own advantages and disadvantages.

Wood. Wood panel garage doors are the most popular choice for residential use. They are available in price ranges to match any wallet and in a wide choice of sectional designs. Wood doors are often fitted with glass inserts to provide interior natural light. (Placement of the windows in the top section adds an additional degree of privacy while still admitting a flood of light.) Wood doors are also made with a polyfoam core which provides an insulating R-value of better than 5. Such insulated doors are highly recommended for heated or attached garages.

Wood garage doors must receive the same treatment as other exterior wood parts of your house. They must be painted or stained regularly, especially the bottom edge, to keep up their appearance and to protect them from the weather.

Fiberglass. Garage doors of fiberglass are much lighter than wood or steel models and therefore are easier to lift. Available in several permanent colors, they require no painting and are virtually maintenance-free. They clean with a hosing, and they stay in balance since they neither absorb nor lose moisture like wood. The fiberglass is translucent, too, letting in outside light to provide a soft pleasant glow, much like a giant skylight.

Aluminum. Aluminum garage doors are lightweight, but are ruggedly durable. While most are factory-finished in white, some are available that can be painted any color you desire. Aluminum doors are made in both one-piece and sectional styles.

Steel. Made of corrosion-resistant, galvanized steel, these doors are unusually durable under all weather conditions. For strength and maximum garage door security, steel is hard to beat. They can be painted to match or complement your home exterior. Overhead steel doors are usually available in only the one-piece style.

WINDOW DESIGN POSSIBILITIES WITH OVERHEAD DOORS

EXAMPLES OF CUSTOMIZING A GARAGE DOOR

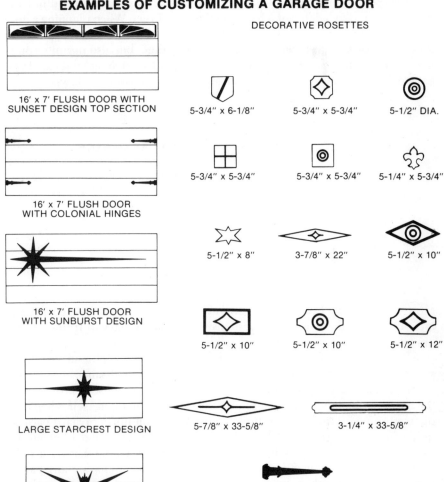

DECORATIVE ROSETTES

16' x 7' FLUSH DOOR WITH
SUNSET DESIGN TOP SECTION

5-3/4" x 6-1/8"

5-3/4" x 5-3/4"

5-1/2" DIA.

5-3/4" x 5-3/4"

5-3/4" x 5-3/4"

5-1/4" x 5-3/4"

16' x 7' FLUSH DOOR
WITH COLONIAL HINGES

5-1/2" x 8"

3-7/8" x 22"

5-1/2" x 10"

16' x 7' FLUSH DOOR
WITH SUNBURST DESIGN

5-1/2" x 10"

5-1/2" x 10"

5-1/2" x 12"

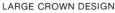

LARGE STARCREST DESIGN

5-7/8" x 33-5/8"

3-1/4" x 33-5/8"

LARGE CROWN DESIGN

4-5/8" x 23-3/4"

Door sizes. Standard stock size doors are usually available in widths from 8 to 18 feet and in heights of 6 feet, 6 inches and 7 feet. When planning a door opening, make it as wide as possible. A wider opening not only gives you freer movement of your vehicle in and out of the garage, but also permits you to move other items in and out without the danger of scratching your car. Typical stock sizes for most garage door manufacturers are as follows:

SINGLE-CAR GARAGE		TWO-CAR GARAGE	
WIDTH	HEIGHT	WIDTH	HEIGHT
8' 0"	6' 8" or 7' 0"	15' 0"	6' 8" or 7' 0"
9' 0"	6' 8" or 7' 0"	16' 0"	6' 8" or 7' 0"
10' 0"	6' 8" or 7' 0"	18' 0"	6' 8" or 7' 0"
12' 0"	6' 8" or 7' 0"		

Most manufacturers will make custom-size garage doors to fit special openings, but these doors are quite expensive. It usually pays to frame out the opening to a stock size, if at all possible.

While measuring for a new garage door or a replacement for an old one, be sure to check the inside headroom. A specific minimum distance between the overhead structure in the garage and the top of the door must be provided for the hardware, counterbalancing mechanisms, and the door itself when in an open position. While, for example, most stock roll-up door hardware requires headroom of at least 10 inches for single-car doors and 12 inches for two-car doors, special low-headroom designs are available that reduce the space needed to about 6 inches. Therefore, before purchasing any garage door, be sure to check the manufacturer's specifications for the needed headroom, as well as necessary sideroom—the space from the side of the door opening to the wall.

INSTALLING AN OVERHEAD GARAGE DOOR. Proper preparation of the garage door opening is most important if the door is to operate satisfactorily. As already mentioned, the finished opening, including outside casing, side jambs, and header, should be the correct size for the door. This opening in both width and height must be kept uniform for the entire opening. That is, the width dimension must be the same at the top, middle, and bottom of the opening; the height dimension must be the same at both sides and the middle.

The plumbness of the opening must also be checked. This can be done easily by running two strings diagonally from the top to the bottom corners. If the strings touch at the point in the center where they pass each other, the opening is plumb.

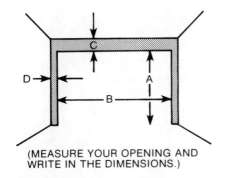

(MEASURE YOUR OPENING AND WRITE IN THE DIMENSIONS.)

A. DOOR OPENING HEIGHT ___FT. ___IN.

B. DOOR OPENING WIDTH ___FT. ___IN.

The important dimensions when ordering any garage door are A and B. With the roll-up type, be sure to have at least 10 inches of headroom clearance (C) for single overhead doors and 12 inches for double doors. There should be at least 4 inches of sideroom (D). Headroom is that space from the door opening header to an overhead structure. Sideroom is that space from the side of the opening to the wall.

Door installation. Manufacturers supply detailed instruction sheets for the installation of their particular garage door. However, here's an example of the step-by-step procedure for installing a typical four-section, roll-up type garage door:

1. Unpack all the hardware and check it against the manufacturer's shipping list. Warranty fulfillment on many wood doors requires painting or staining before installation. New doors should be treated with a wood preservative before priming. Use an oil-base exterior primer on all the edges, as well as inside and out. Allow this coat to dry about 36 to 48 hours before you apply the finish coat. Whatever finish you use, apply it as directed on the container.

2. Fasten the bolts in the door sections to the hinges and hangers. Insert the track rollers into the hangers. If required, now is the time to attach the U-bar brace.

3. To assemble the door, place the bottom door section in the door opening and check for level. Place the second door section on the first and attach with the hinges and hangers. Do this with each door section, but don't attach the top roller hanger just yet.

4. Place the vertical tracks over the rollers, align, and bolt the track firmly to the door jamb. Fasten the vertical track, the curved track, and the horizontal track to the jamb angle at the top of the door. The entire track assembly is now installed.

5. Temporarily secure the horizontal track to the ceiling or joists, and install the top roller hangers in the upper corners of the top door section. Cautiously test the door's action and alignment by raising it to about half-opening. Track alignment corrections should be made at this time.

6. Attach the angle iron support between each track's end and a nearby ceiling joist. A cross brace may be added to support the iron and increase its holding power.

7. Raise the door onto the horizontal track and secure it in place. Attach the springs and cables. Make the final adjustments: Set the spring tension, check

Before installing overhead door, provide all necessary jambs (left). Fasten the lower track to the back jamb with lag screws (right).

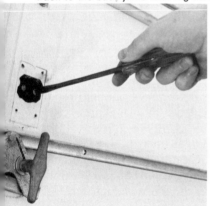

Fasten all hardware to door sections (left). Check the door lock mechanism to be sure it works properly (right).

After installing rollers, insert the first door section in the track (left). Once first section is level, all others can be inserted in track (right).

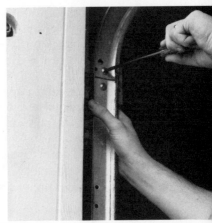

Sections can be fastened together by bolting hinge hardware (left). Install the upper section of the track and fasten it at the rear (right).

Carefully install the springs. Remember, they can be dangerous (left). The spring cable can be tied as directed by the manufacturer (right).

Fasten stop around the door to prevent drafts (left). The completed door. The door should ride along the track (right).

the rollers, install the door lock and locking bars, and tighten the nuts and bolts. Keep in mind that loose hinges will cause the rollers to bend, while rollers too tight in the track will also bind. If the locking bars do not glide freely through their openings, the guides at the edge of each side of the door can be adjusted. The spring tension of an extension spring can be adjusted by shortening the cable or by taking up the slack. The torsion type of spring is adjusted by loosening the locknut and winding the spring tighter with a bar inserted in the collar. **NOTE:** Garage door springs under tension can be dangerous; when installing or adjusting, use extreme care. Never stand in front of or behind a tensioned spring while working on it.

8. To complete the installation, close the door and attach vertical wood stop strips to the side frame. Also nail a horizontal stop strip to the top of the

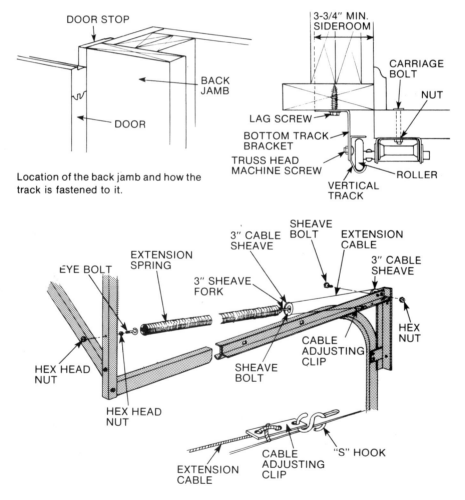

Location of the back jamb and how the track is fastened to it.

The upper track section and how its hardware is connected together.

door frame. If the floor of the garage is not level at the opening, the new door won't close flush. This difficulty can be overcome simply by attaching a strip of special garage door weatherstripping along the bottom edge that will seal the uneven space.

Maintenance of overhead garage doors. The only maintenance required by overhead garage doors is an occasional lubrication of all moving parts with oil or powdered graphite. Be sure that the inside of the tracks and the roller bearings are kept clean and are well-oiled. Lubricate the moving parts of the lock at least once a year with powdered graphite—never use oil.

Straighten any nicks or bends that should appear in the track. Check the track occasionally with a level to be sure that it is plumb. To adjust the track, loosen the bolts and tap the bracket with a plastic or leather mallet or a block of wood. Once the track is plumb, tighten the bolts. If the door springs have been weakened or damaged, replacement is the only solution.

AUTOMATIC GARAGE DOOR OPERATOR. Convenience is pressing the button of your radio control from the comfort of your car and watching the automatic garage door operator open the door and turn on the light. Drive in and press the button again (or the wall switch). The door shuts behind you—and locks. A time-delay switch leaves the operator light on until you've had an opportunity to get out of the car and into the house. It turns off automatically in about 1-1/2 or 2 minutes.

Automatic garage door operators give you protection, too—protection from the wind and weather, plus protection from prowlers. They protect the garage contents when you leave because it's so easy to close the door with a push of the button. Most operators feature a return switch which causes the automatic reversal of the door when it encounters an obstruction during its downward movement.

Most residential automatic door openers will operate with any type of overhead garage door type—roll-up sectional, one-piece with tracks, and one-piece trackless. When selecting the opener unit for your garage door, check the manufacturer's specifications to make certain there is sufficient headroom and back space (the area between the back of the opener and garage wall). Also check the high-rise, or the distance between the highest arc of the door travel and the garage ceiling. Most openers require at least 3-inch clearance.

Before installing the opener, make sure that the door operates properly and that all moving parts are well lubricated. The present lock must be made inoperable by jamming it in the open position or by cutting off the lock bar ends so they can't engage the slots in the track. The door opener could be ruined if it tried to open when the garage door was locked. Of course, it's not necessary to lock the door since a door equipped with an automatic operator can't be opened manually from outside the garage. If an electrical failure occurs, most openers can be operated manually from inside the garage.

HOW AUTOMATIC GARAGE DOOR OPENER IS ASSEMBLED

To assemble a door opener, put the power track together (left). Fasten the chain connector to the chain, using the link assembly (right).

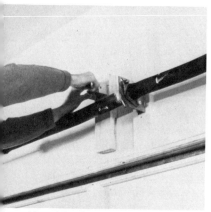

Mount the front wall bracket above the center of the door (left). Connect power track to the wall bracket (right).

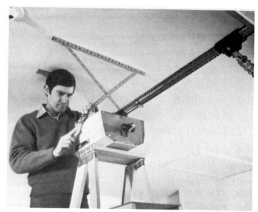

Support power unit with stepladder, while mounting ceiling bracket (left). Fasten the hanger to the ceiling bracket and to the power unit (right) (Courtesy of The Stanley Works).

Attach the door mounting bracket to the door (left) and the power track (right).

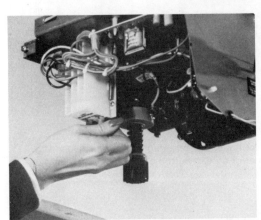 

Remove cover and take out transmitter pack (left). Adjust the transmitter according to manufacturer's directions (right).

Replace pack and plug in power unit. Check opener operation (left). Replace cover, add light bulbs, and opener is ready for use (right) (Courtesy of The Stanley Works).

When it comes to the actual installation of the automatic garage door operator, be sure to carefully follow the manufacturer's directions given in the owner's manual. Once the unit is installed, check its operation before mailing in the warranty card to the manufacturer.

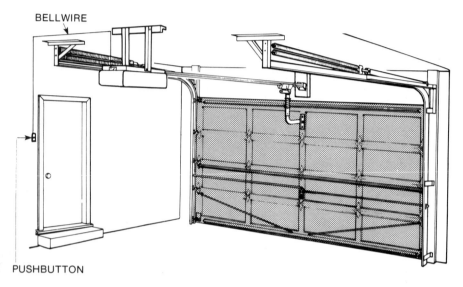

Completed installation of a garage door opener. The garage door can be opened by either a remote control unit in the car or a push-button on the inside garage wall.

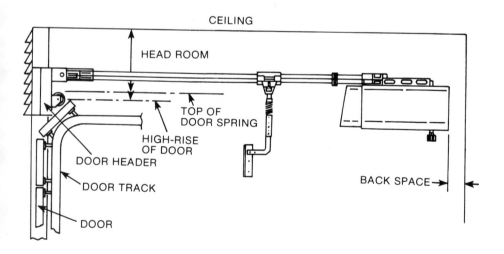

The important dimensions to consider when purchasing a garage door opener.

Troubleshooting a door operator. If electrical problems with the operator can't be determined or remedied, the electrical assembly may be easily removed and returned for repair or replacement. To remove, disconnect the push-button and radio wires, the power source leads or plug-in cord, and the five wires to the terminal board of the electrical assembly from motor and lamp(s). Then remove the mounting screws and carefully remove the electrical assembly. Here are some common problems that occur with typical automatic operators and their possible solutions.

PROBLEM	POSSIBLE CAUSE	SOLUTION
Operates from push-button but won't operate from hand transmitter control.	Weak battery.	Replace battery.
	Transmitter or receiver inoperable.	Check wires from receiver. Return receiver with transmitter for repair.
Won't open or close from radio or push-button.	Blown house fuse.	Check line fuse.
	Open circuit breaker in the motor.	Allow few minutes for motor to cool off and try again.
	Defective lamp timer.	Replace.
	Defective capacitor.	Replace.
	Defective relay.	Replace.
	Defective transformer.	Replace.
	Defective motor.	Replace.
	Door binding.	Repair and/or adjust.
Reduced operating range of radio control.	Weak battery.	Replace.
	Transmitter or receiver out of adjustment.	Return receiver with transmitter for adjustment.
	Too cold.	Batteries tend to lose power in extremely cold weather.
Unexpected (phantom) operation (door goes up and down on its own).	Radio control.	Return receiver with transmitter for repair.
	Push-button.	Repair or replace.
	Staple through push-button wire causing short circuit.	Remove staple.
Light does not work.	Bulb.	Replace.
	Lamp timer.	Replace.
	Light socket.	Replace.

PROBLEM	POSSIBLE CAUSE	SOLUTION
Door makes one operation either up or down, operator stops running and will not start again when radio or wall push-button is pressed. (Disconnect power line from operator and immediately reconnect again. Operator makes one more complete cycle.)	Shorted push-button wires or radio control receiver wires. Defective push-button. Defective radio control receiver.	Repair. Replace. Return receiver with transmitter for repair.
Does not open or close fully.	Door force adjustments too sensitive. Door track out of line. Broken door roller. Door spring out of adjustment. Limit finger (close only).	Adjust. Adjust. Replace. Adjust or replace. Adjust.
Door won't reverse when meeting an obstruction.	"Close" limit guide bar on top of power head sticking (does not release leaf switch when door is partially open). Solenoid and switch assembly defective.	Loosen pivot hexnut 1/8 turn. Replace.

8 | Attaching A Carport To Your Home

A CARPORT—whether attached or free-standing—is the easiest home to build for your car. If you've converted your garage into an attractive living space or a good-size workshop, it's often possible to locate a carport in front of the old garage. This makes it possible to use the in-place driveway. Or, you may place the carport on the side of the house and make the cover an extension of the existing roof lines. This makes it possible to use the in-place driveway. If this isn't feasible, a frequent solution is erecting a shed-type structure against a wall of the house.

Either way, construction procedures can be minimized by viewing the carport as a husky frame that is there to support a roof. Actually, there are three major phases in building a carport: laying a slab, building supporting posts, and adding a roof.

Wood screen shields the attached carport, giving it a pleasant court effect.

An attached carport shelters the car and, in rainy weather, serves as a children's play area.

(Above) An attached carport can be extended to furnish a dining area as well as storage space. (Below) The carport can be placed in front of the house with pleasing results.

Laying a slab. Lay out the edges of the slab with string lines as described on page 34; check for square by measuring diagonally across from corner to corner. When dimensions are the same on each diagonal, the slab will be square. Remember that the slab must line up with the walls of the existing house, and if it is to be poured against the foundation, the slab must be secured to the old structure as discussed in Chapter 3.

Level the edge of the slab against the house, 4 to 6 inches below the siding or top of the foundation wall. Slope the front end of the form down and away from the house for drainage, 2 inches for each 10 feet. Dig a 1-foot wide trench to a depth below the local frost line on three sides of the slab to act as the footer; the house's foundation will perform this task on the fourth side of the slab. Excavate the remaining area of slab to a depth of 4 to 6 inches and fill with pit-run gravel or crushed rock. In areas where the ground freezes, reinforce the concrete with 6- by-6 welded steel mesh or 3/8-inch reinforcing bars crisscrossed on 12-inch centers.

Fill the form with concrete (1 part portland cement, 3 parts sand, 4 parts gravel, and minimum water) and strike off the level with a straight-edged 2-by-4 across the top of the form. As soon as the concrete begins to set, finish the surface with a wood float first. A smooth finish is desired; then steel trowel the surface. Work from the plank bridge across the floor area. Use an edger around the sides and a groover to make a rectangular pattern, if desired. Insert 1/2-inch anchor bolts or post base clips into the concrete slab at each post location.

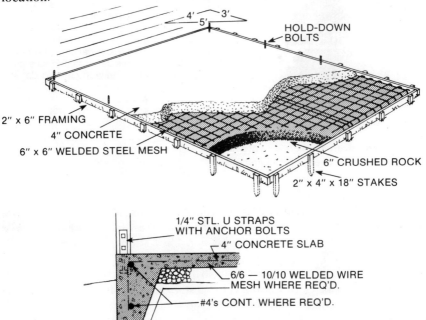

Proper way to set forms and pour the concrete for a carport slab. The slab should be tied into the house foundation as described in Chapter 3. The "U" strap shown in detail above may be used in place of the hold-down bolts or post base clamp.

The carport can be built without pouring a slab—a thick bed of well-tamped gravel which can also be a lead-in from the driveway. If so, the posts must be supported with adequate concrete footings. The advantages of a slab are obvious—easy maintenance and a good floor for occasional use as a ping-pong court, etc.

Carport with a shed roof. The 4-by-4-inch support posts must be anchored to the slab. If steel dowels were set into the slab, drill 1/2-inch holes in the bottom posts and set them into position over the steel dowels. Anchor bolts are usually used in conjunction with post base clips. To install such a clip, secure its base with the anchor bolt, put the spacer in place, put the 4-by-4-inch post on the spacer, wrap-up the slotted base, and nail it with 10-gauge barbed nails. If you didn't put anchor bolts into the slab, the clip base can be attached with concrete nails through the bottom holes.

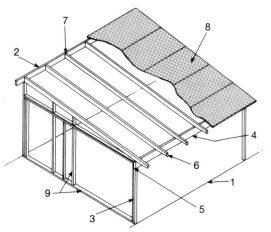

1 New Concrete Slab
2 2" x 6" Ledger spiked or lag screwed to studs of house wall
3 4" x 4" Posts
4 2" x 12" Header Beam
5 Post Cap (Readymade connector)
6 2" x 6" Joist/Rafters
7 Joist Hangers
8 Plywood Roof Sheathing to support finish roofing.
9 Optional—standard framing to fill in sides. Treated sole plate attached with case-hardened nails or with anchor bolts that were set in place when the concrete was poured.

Simplified construction drawing of shed type attached carport. The same basic construction can be used when opening is in front rather than on side.

The 2-by-12-inch can be used as the front header for most attached carports and it can be fastened to the front support post with 4-inch angle brackets or beam clips, nailed or screwed to the header. The bottom of the header should be a minimum of 7 feet, 4 inches from the slab.

A 2-by-6-inch back header or ledger strip is fastened to the studs or the wall of the house. For brick or masonry, use a star drill or masonry bit and insert lead shields or tampons. For frame or stucco walls, fasten the ledger strip with nails or lag screws to the studs of the house wall. To determine the proper height of the roof, allow a 1-inch minimum pitch per foot of distance between the front and rear headers for adequate drainage.

The 2-by-6-inch rafters, set 2 feet on centers, should be held in position against the rear header and fastened in place with commercial metal joist hangers. The front portion of the rafters may either be set on the header or for a neater appearance, be notched. Once the rafters are installed, apply the plywood roof sheathing to support the finish roofing. To eliminate edge blocking, use panel clips. Insert these clips between the panels of plywood, centered between the rafters.

Cover the roof sheathing with 15-pound roofing felt turned over at the edges and covered with a 1-by-2 trim strip. Space 3/4-inch footing nails 6 inches apart. Apply the roof by first nailing a 9-inch starter strip along the eave and sides. Brush adhesive cement on the starter strip and apply the first course of shingle roll roofing, overlapping the eave and trim strips at the sides 1/2 inch all around. Nail through the top selvage. Apply succeeding courses by cementing the lower edge and nailing the top selvage. For flashing, use copper, aluminum, or galvanized steel slipped under the wood or shingle siding, or bent into routed-out brick joint. Nails through the bent-over flange hold the flashing in the joint. Fill the joint with asphalt mastic. Counterflash the brick walls.

Many people prefer to build their carport roof of corrugated fiberglass plastic or polyester panels. They are durable and attractive and, being translucent, they permit light to fill the carport area. Both light and warmth are transmitted in accordance with the particular color selected. For warmer locations, colors with lower transmission values are recommended. The table below will help you determine the most suitable color for your carport roof. This color, of course, should be complementary to those of your house.

TRANSMISSION VALUE					
Color	% Light	% Heat	Color	% Light	% Heat
Skylite Green	69—77	61—67	Gold	43—48	54—58
Lime	37—42	34—38	Desert Sand	45—54	55—64
Teal Blue	37—42	34—38	Yellow	59—65	41—44
Emerald	36—44	50—54	Sea Green	52—58	60—68
White	56—61	31—34	Clear	78—83	63—67

When using plastic panels for a carport roof, it is necessary to place cross braces, the same lumber size as the rafters, every 3 to 4 feet. The cross bracing should be nailed or screwed directly to the rafters. The top edge of the bracing and rafters must be flush.

After all the bracing is in place, nail corrugated redwood or rubber molding on the headers and cross braces, and nail crested molding strips on the rafters. Now paint or stain all the framework before installing the fiberglass plastic panels. When the finish is dry, lay the first panel on the corner away from the

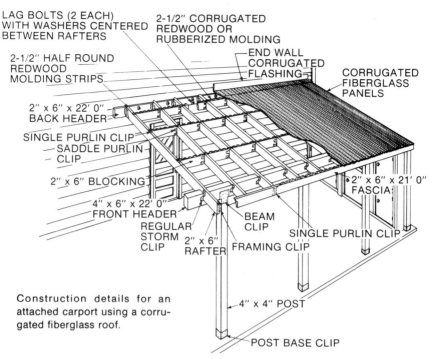

LAG BOLTS (2 EACH) WITH WASHERS CENTERED BETWEEN RAFTERS

2-1/2" CORRUGATED REDWOOD OR RUBBERIZED MOLDING

2-1/2" HALF ROUND REDWOOD MOLDING STRIPS

END WALL CORRUGATED FLASHING

CORRUGATED FIBERGLASS PANELS

2" x 6" x 22' 0" BACK HEADER

SINGLE PURLIN CLIP
—SADDLE PURLIN CLIP

2" x 6" BLOCKING

2" x 6" x 21' 0" FASCIA

4" x 6" x 22' 0" FRONT HEADER

REGULAR STORM CLIP

BEAM CLIP

SINGLE PURLIN CLIP

2" x 6" RAFTER

FRAMING CLIP

Construction details for an attached carport using a corrugated fiberglass roof.

4" x 4" POST

POST BASE CLIP

usual wind direction, so that the wind will blow over, not under, the overlapped panels. Most manufacturers recommend the use of a liquid mastic between the molding and the panel for a watertight seal.

When all panels are in place, square them up evenly and nail at the crown of the corrugation; every 12 inches along the rafters; and every second or third corrugation along the bracing. It is best to predrill all holes with a 1/8-inch drill bit to avoid craze marks. Use aluminum screw-grip nails and neoprene washers, as recommended by the manufacturer.

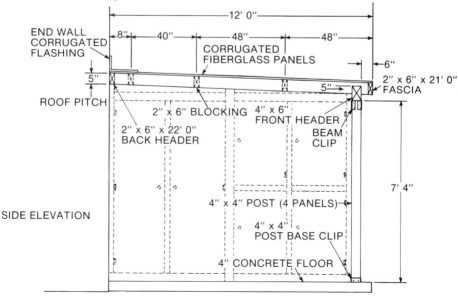

12' 0"

END WALL CORRUGATED FLASHING

8"   40"   48"   48"

CORRUGATED FIBERGLASS PANELS

6"

5"

5"

2" x 6" x 21' 0" FASCIA

ROOF PITCH

2" x 6" BLOCKING

4" x 6" FRONT HEADER

2" x 6" x 22' 0" BACK HEADER

BEAM CLIP

7' 4"

4" x 4" POST (4 PANELS)

SIDE ELEVATION

4" x 4" POST BASE CLIP

4" CONCRETE FLOOR

116

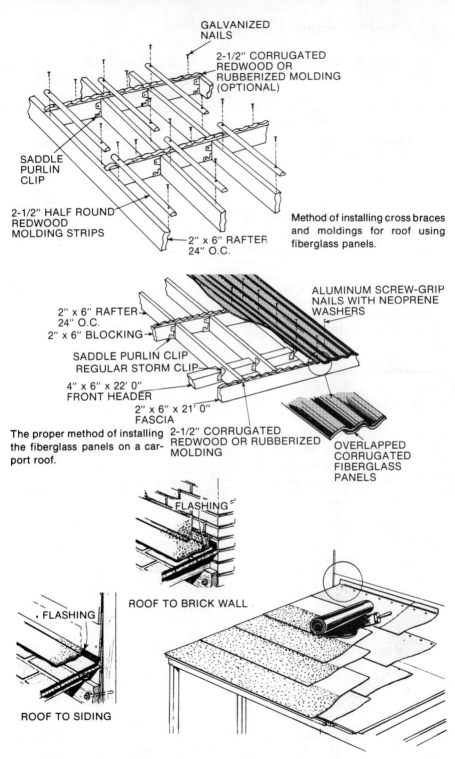

GALVANIZED
NAILS

2-1/2" CORRUGATED
REDWOOD OR
RUBBERIZED MOLDING
(OPTIONAL)

SADDLE
PURLIN
CLIP

2-1/2" HALF ROUND
REDWOOD
MOLDING STRIPS

2" x 6" RAFTER
24" O.C.

Method of installing cross braces and moldings for roof using fiberglass panels.

2" x 6" RAFTER
24" O.C.
2" x 6" BLOCKING

SADDLE PURLIN CLIP
REGULAR STORM CLIP

4" x 6" x 22' 0"
FRONT HEADER

2" x 6" x 21' 0"
FASCIA

2-1/2" CORRUGATED
REDWOOD OR RUBBERIZED
MOLDING

ALUMINUM SCREW-GRIP
NAILS WITH NEOPRENE
WASHERS

OVERLAPPED
CORRUGATED
FIBERGLASS
PANELS

The proper method of installing the fiberglass panels on a carport roof.

FLASHING

ROOF TO BRICK WALL

FLASHING

ROOF TO SIDING

Application of roll roofing to attached carport roof

117

The sidewall or back of attached carports are often wholly or partially closed in with simple cabinetry done with exterior grades of plywood. Thus, the project can provide storage space and car protection. Conventional framing, discussed later in this chapter, can be used to fill in the sides. A treated sole or base plate should be attached to the slab with case-hardened steel concrete nails or with anchor bolts or clips that were set in place when the concrete was poured. More on storage units for carports can be found in Chapter 9.

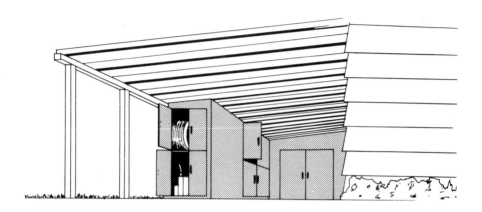

Storage areas such as this can easily be built into a shed-roof carport.

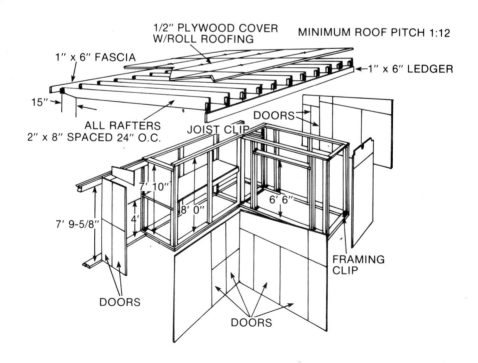

Carport with a gable roof. The slab and posts are set in the same manner as for the shed roof construction. The back two posts should fasten to the house with nails, lag screws, or lead anchor bolts. The 4-by-12-inch beams on the sides and front of the carport should be placed on the posts and held by heavy metal angles, using screws or bolts as fasteners.

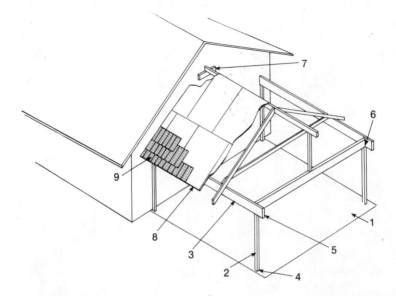

1 New Concrete Slab
2 4" x 4" Posts
3 4" x 12" Beams
4 Post Anchors—some made for installation when concrete is poured. Others may be added after concrete sets.
5 Heavy Metal Angles—use screws or bolts as fasteners.
6 Beam Hangers
7 Support for New Ridge—spike to studs of existing wall or use beam hanger.
8 Plywood Roof Sheathing is base for finish roofing.
9 Shingles

Simplified construction drawing of an attached gable roof carport. Note that this has a ridge board which is constructed in the same manner as described in Chapter 3.

A 1-by-8-inch ridge board is fastened to a 2-by-6 cleat, fastened to the studs in the house. It is also held by a 2-by-4 support connected to the front beam. The rafters, which are usually spaced 24 inches on centers, can be cut to length with the proper angle cut at the ridge and eave, and with notches provided for the side beams. The desired roof pitch—which should be the same as the house or at least complement it—determines the eave angle at which to cut the rafter ends. The pitch also determines the angle of the notches to get 3-inch contacts with the beams. Put up the back rafter first, fastening it to the house studs wherever possible. The front rafter is installed next. The top edge of each rafter should be level with the top of the ridge board. Toenail each rafter to the ridge board with 8d nails, then secure the other end to the beam with 16d nails. Put the remaining rafters up a pair at a time, checking the ridge board occasionally as you go along to make sure it remains level. Nail 2-by-4 cross ties to every other rafter to prevent any tendency the beams may have to move inward or outward.

After the sheathing is applied, place a layer of 15-pound felt over it. Follow this with a double-thickness of shingles as the lowest course. Overhang the shingles 1/2 inch at the eaves and 1/4 inch at the front gable to form a drip edge. Be sure to use flashing between the old and new structures to keep the weather out. Drive 1-inch galvanized roofing nails 1/2 inch above the slots in the shingles and 1 inch to the side of each shingle's centerline. The bottom of each course should just cover the ends of the slots in the previous course. A metal cap strip covers the ridge.

Step-by-step procedure for applying asphalt shingles to a hipped-roof carport. The color of the roofing should be the same as the remaining portion of the house.

Carport and patio shelter. A carport and covered patio shelter can be attached to the rear or side of the home. An addition like this will keep your car out of the weather and provide shelter and storage for your patio and garden equipment.

Basic steps in building a carport/patio shelter as described in text (Courtesy of American Plywood Assoc.).

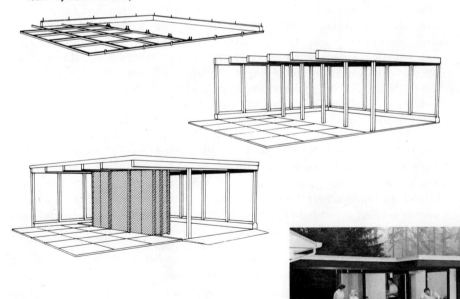

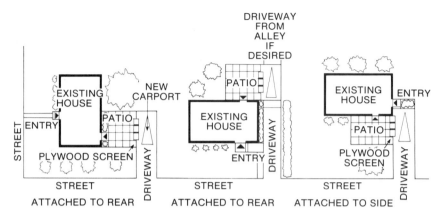

Various ways to locate the carport/patio shelter on your property. The carport/patic shelter can also be built as a freestanding unit at the rear of the yard.

To lay out the slab, follow the general procedure described earlier in this chapter and in Chapter 3. When slab layout is considered square, dig a 2-foot wide trench to a depth below the local frost line for the foundation wall along the rear and right side. Dig 2-foot square holes at each post footing location. Now set batter boards approximately 2 feet out from the corners and the intersection of the post line with the rear wall and the front edge of the slab. Stretch strings to locate the outside face of the foundation wall and the post line. Check for square again by taping the diagonals to the corners where the strings intersect. Then, stake the 2-by-6s on edge for the footings along the rear and right side. Build the wall forms for the foundation to the required height with 2-by-4s and plywood or shiplap. Set the outside form panels on the top edge of the 2-by-6 footing forms and nail them into position with the inside face lined up with the batter board strings. Set the inside form panels so that the forms are 6 inches apart. Install one row of form ties about halfway up from the top of the footing and nail the wood bracing on 2-by-4s across the top where required. Install wood spreaders between the forms as needed. Build bottomless boxes for the post footings from 2-by-6 scrap lumber. Assemble 6-by-6-inch plinth forms from scrap shiplap and nail them to the 2-by-4s fastened across the post footing forms. Pour concrete into the forms and then insert a post base clip into the concrete foundation at each post location. Insert the plinths into the clip at each post footing. The 2-by-4 plates should be pressure treated with a water repellent.

Using a carpenter's level, set the plates on top of the freshly poured wall with 20d nails driven into the bottom side to act as plate anchors. Remove the formwork after the concrete has sufficiently hardened. Cut 4-by-4-inch posts to length; fasten with 1/2-inch lag screws to the metal clips. Also, position and fasten the posts to the straps from the footing plinths. Now nail a 2-by-4 continuous plate across the posts on the right carport wall. Cut 4-by-10-inch beams to length and fasten to the top plate with metal joist anchors on both sides of

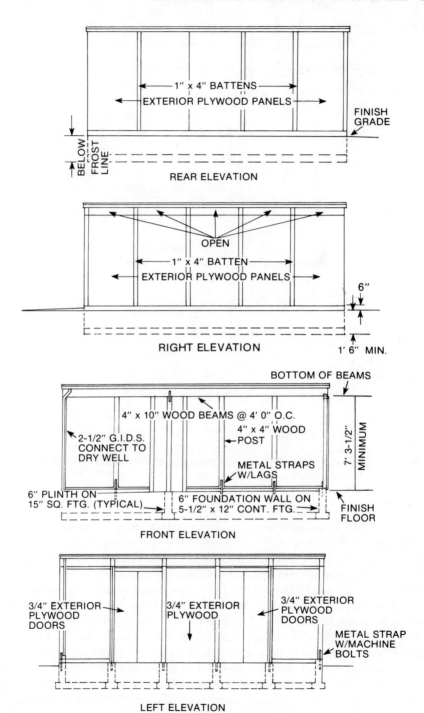

Elevation details of the carport/patio shelter.

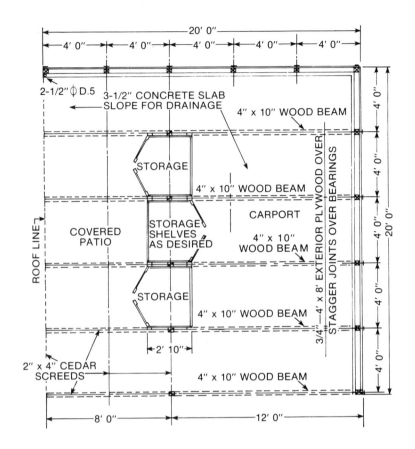

Roof layout and slab details of the carport/patio shelter. When applying the plywood sheathing over the wood beam, be sure to stagger the joints over the bearing surfaces.

each beam. Use galvanized metal tie straps and nails in other locations where the beams are connected directly to posts. Keep the beams aligned with temporary bracing across the tops. It would be well at this stage of construction to apply two coats of stain to all the beams, posts, and plates.

Prime both the sides and the edges of the exterior plywood wall panels with a suitable primer before installation. When the primer is dry, fasten to the posts, plates, and beams with 8d noncorrosive box or casing nails, 6 inches on center along all edges. After applying a coat of primer to the "A" face and edges of the 3/4-inch exterior plywood roof panels, fasten them to the tops of the beams with the end edges staggered. Use aluminum panel clips at 16-inch centers and fasten the panels with 8d common nails 6 inches on center along the edges at the bearings. Install 2-by-2-inch blocking between the beams at the outside edges to provide nailing for the 1-by-3-inch fir fascia which should be back primed before installation.

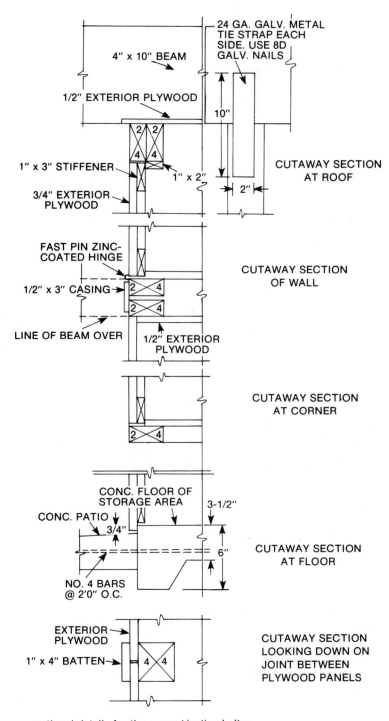

24 GA. GALV. METAL TIE STRAP EACH SIDE. USE 8D GALV. NAILS

4″ x 10″ BEAM

1/2″ EXTERIOR PLYWOOD

10″

CUTAWAY SECTION AT ROOF

1″ x 3″ STIFFENER

1″ x 2″

2″

3/4″ EXTERIOR PLYWOOD

FAST PIN ZINC-COATED HINGE

CUTAWAY SECTION OF WALL

1/2″ x 3″ CASING

LINE OF BEAM OVER

1/2″ EXTERIOR PLYWOOD

CUTAWAY SECTION AT CORNER

CONC. FLOOR OF STORAGE AREA

3-1/2″

CONC. PATIO

3/4″

6″

CUTAWAY SECTION AT FLOOR

NO. 4 BARS @ 2′0″ O.C.

EXTERIOR PLYWOOD

1″ x 4″ BATTEN

CUTAWAY SECTION LOOKING DOWN ON JOINT BETWEEN PLYWOOD PANELS

Door and screen sectional details for the carport/patio shelter.

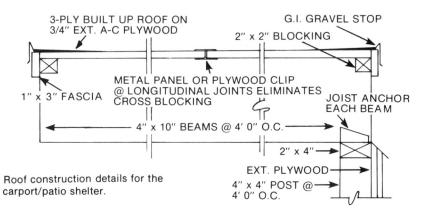

Roof construction details for the carport/patio shelter.

Application of the built-up roof is the next step. Call in a professional roof applicator for this job. He can recommend the best and most economical roof to meet the requirements in your locality. Have the roofer or a sheet metal shop make up and install the shop-primed galvanized gravel stop to insure a neat installation.

Prepare for the pouring and finishing of the patio and carport slab by setting 2-by-4 cedar screeds in a 4-by-4-foot pattern. Set the screeds to effect a slope of approximately 1/8 inch: 1 to 0 inches from the rear to the front of the carport and the same from the front of the storage cabinets to the edge of the patio slab. The edge of the slab at the storage cabinet fronts is deepened, and reinforcing steel is installed at 24-inch centers to keep the slab from cracking at this point. To finish the carport and patio slab, use a broom finish, which is accomplished by carefully dragging a stiff broom across the surface as the concrete begins to set. If a pebbled texture is desired for the patio, brush the concrete with a stiff broom approximately 4 hours after pouring and hose off the top surface of cement particles using generous amounts of clean water.

Construction of the storage cabinets is one of the last steps. Use 1/2-inch exterior plywood for the walls, partitions, and roof with 2-by-4s at the outside corners for additional strength. Double 2-by-4s over door openings act as headers between double 2-by-4 spacers at post locations. The doors are made of 3/4-inch exterior plywood with 1-by-3-inch fir stiffeners along all edges— nailed and glued. The edges of the 1/2-inch plywood partitions act as stops along the jambs. Nail a 1-by-2 to the header at the top to form a stop. Hang the doors with a pair of zinc-coated fast pin butts and install suitable catches and hasps. Install shelving to suit.

Use a good quality exterior house paint and stain on your new structure. Over the prime undercoat apply two coats of exterior house paint on all plywood surfaces, fascia board, and metal gravel stop. A colorful motif may be achieved by painting the wall panels and storage cabinet doors in alternate harmonizing colors. After the paint has thoroughly dried, apply 1-by-4 wood battens (prestained with two coats) over the plywood joints at each post location on the rear and right side walls. Fasten with 8d galvanized nails and set slightly below the surface.

Sundeck-carport. Expand your living space indoors and out, if you need more room, with a sundeck-carport addition. The carport doubles as a sundeck—a secluded area adjacent to second-floor rooms for sunbathing and relaxation.

An attractive sundeck can be constructed over the carport. All you need is a second floor opening (Courtesy of Western Wood Products Assoc.).

Carport/sundeck built in front of a converted garage.

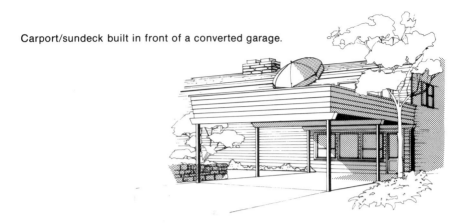

Build the structure on a concrete slab, with footings for the posts to suit local frost conditions and building codes. Use 4-by-6-inch posts at the house wall and front of the structure, with 4-by-14 beams across. At the center, 6-by-6-inch posts support a 6-by-14 beam. Joists are 2-by-6s and extend past the beams so that the 2-by-4 railing uprights can be nailed to them. Along the other two sides, these uprights are bolted to doubled joists as shown in the side section. Be sure the roof has adequate pitch for drainage.

Before the roof area is used as a deck area, it must be made "traffic-proof" so that wear will not cause leaks. Since most flat-type roofs that would be used for deck purposes are usually already covered with a webbing of impregnated felt, tar, or asphalt and gravel, or simply a layer of 90-pound felt rolled roofing, an additional built-up arrangement must be provided to withstand the traffic.

Where the roof slope exceeds a 1/4 inch per foot pitch, to provide the necessary drainage you can use anything from 2-by-2s up to 2-by-10s cut on a diagonal across the face to form long wedges or shims to level the deck floor. The "shims" should be spaced at 16-inch intervals, the usual spacing for floor joists. The decking boards—spaced 3/8 to 3/4 inch apart—are then fastened to the shims, or the shims may be used to support square decking platforms. The advantage of the latter is that they may be lifted up at will for roof repairs underneath or for recovery of lost items that may have fallen through. In either case, the outer end of the shims is closed with a fascia of the same material used for the flooring boards. Use an outside railing material and design that will blend the sundeck into the house.

Exterior-grade plywood, special fiberglass deck panels, or fiberglass cloth, as well as specially designed roof decking materials, may also be used as coverings for roof-top decks. These should be installed as directed by their manufacturer. In addition, if your roof is covered with roll roofing, there are several so-called deck coatings that can be painted or sprayed over the surface. While these products will convert the average roof into a suitable deck for sunning, they are not applicable for heavy service.

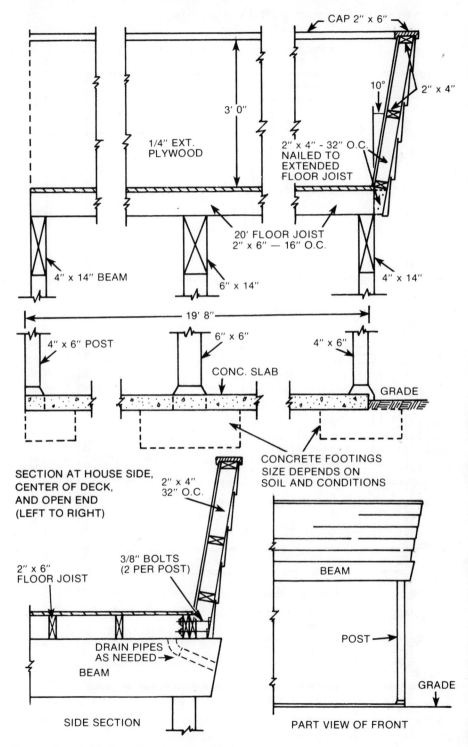

CAP 2" x 6"

10°

2" x 4"

3' 0"

1/4" EXT. PLYWOOD

2" x 4" - 32" O.C. NAILED TO EXTENDED FLOOR JOIST

20' FLOOR JOIST 2" x 6" — 16" O.C.

4" x 14" BEAM

6" x 14"

4" x 14"

19' 8"

4" x 6" POST

6" x 6"

4" x 6"

CONC. SLAB

GRADE

CONCRETE FOOTINGS SIZE DEPENDS ON SOIL AND CONDITIONS

SECTION AT HOUSE SIDE, CENTER OF DECK, AND OPEN END (LEFT TO RIGHT)

2" x 4" 32" O.C.

2" x 6" FLOOR JOIST

3/8" BOLTS (2 PER POST)

DRAIN PIPES AS NEEDED

BEAM

SIDE SECTION

BEAM

POST

GRADE

PART VIEW OF FRONT

Deck and post details for the carport/sundeck.

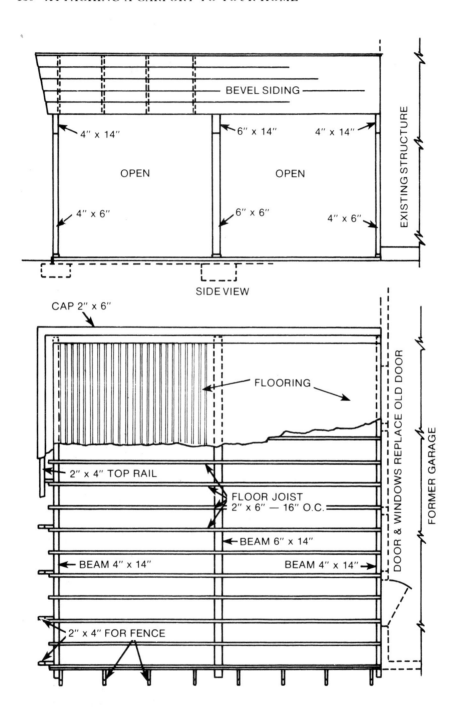

Deck and framing details for the carport/sundeck.

9 | Free-Standing Carports

A WELL-PLANNED, free-standing carport and storage area can give you a low-cost multipurpose space. There is little question that a carport is less expensive than building a conventional garage. As pointed out earlier, garage-less homes are at a major disadvantage in that there is no shelter for the family automobile. While a *simple* carport will provide necessary shelter for any vehicle, it doesn't offer a complete solution to the garage-less problem. Since the *simple* carport is only a concrete slab (or a gravel area) with a roof over it, it doesn't permit the storage of the bulky yard equipment and lawn furniture that needs to be kept out of the rain. If such items are brought under the carport roof, they not only create an ugly clutter, but will soon take over the slab, making it rather hazardous to put the car under *its* shelter. You won't, however, run into this problem if you build any one of the *multipurpose*, free-standing carports illustrated in this chapter.

What do we mean by "multipurpose" carport? It is a carport that serves other functions in addition to furnishing shelter for a car. The carports shown here not only provide storage space for garden tools, lawn furniture, bikes, sporting gear, and other outdoor items, they also feature such things as a workshop, play room, boat port, patio, outdoor living space, play loft, as well as special storage areas. For example, let's take a look at the details of the single carport with workshop and storage area. A shed roof and double corner post lend a charmingly modern air to this carport. About 120 square feet of enclosed space—an area almost 6 feet wide for its full length—gives you room for storing powered garden tools, for parking bicycles, wagons, and other small-fry rolling stock, and for a workshop. Two doors in this enclosure open on the carport area, while a third gives access to the workshop and bicycle storage area from the outside. A wide window sheds light on the workbench.

Another example of a multipurpose storage feature is shown in the double carport that has a shelter for two cars, enclosed storage for gardening and barbecuing needs, plus an area for children's outdoor toys and bikes. The sweeping gable roof on the open beams accents this most attractive modern design. The roof ties run through the storage unit, the rafters themselves being enclosed with a hardboard soffit or ceiling panel. An interior wall separates the storage area into two parts, each with its own door. The exterior walls are finished with sheet plywood siding. And, in keeping with the multipurpose theme, a board fence at the end of one car lane adapts this area for use as a patio or outdoor eating area.

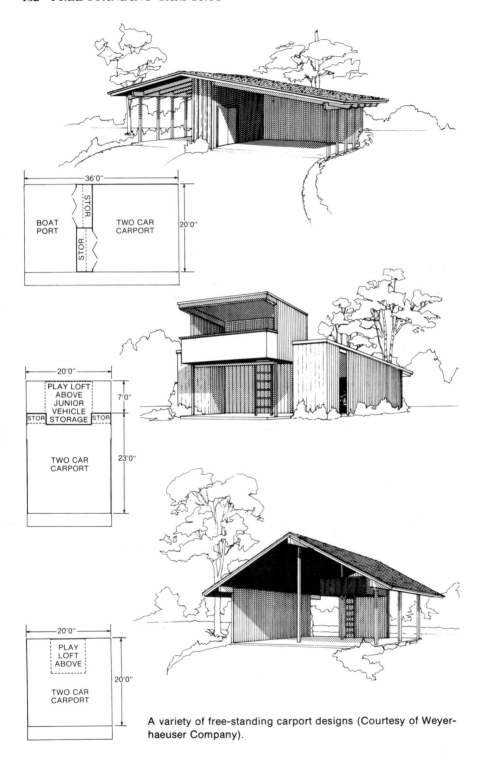

A variety of free-standing carport designs (Courtesy of Weyer-haeuser Company).

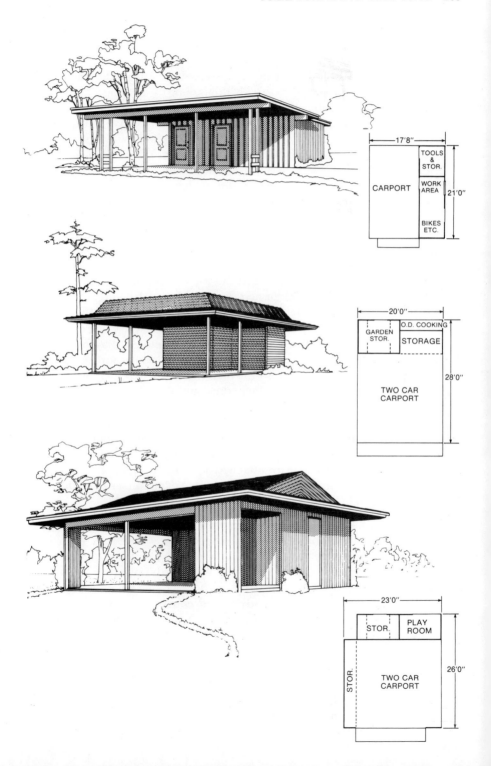

	17'8"	
		TOOLS & STOR.
CARPORT	WORK AREA	21'0"
	BIKES ETC.	

	20'0"	
	GARDEN STOR.	O.D. COOKING / STORAGE
TWO CAR CARPORT		28'0"

	23'0"	
	STOR.	PLAY ROOM
STOR.	TWO CAR CARPORT	26'0"

No matter what extra duties you give your carport, however, it should appear as an integrated part of the house and property. There are several ways to achieve this effect.

1. **Style.** To relate the two structures, style-wise, repeat the lines of the house in the lines of the carport. Usually this is done by creating a similar look in the roof of the carport. Or you can actually match a "period" style, such as colonial, modern, or ranch. Sometimes, by using other ways to tie the house together with the carport, you can contrast period styles very effectively—by putting a modern-lined carport with a colonial house, for instance.

2. **Color.** Bridge the "gap" between the house and carport by using some of the same color in both. The carport doesn't have to be painted exactly as the house is, though it can be. Often, by painting the trim of the carport the same color as the main hues of the house, you can establish a relationship that is strong enough, and the rest of the carport can be in a brand new—but harmonious—shade. Natural wood stains are also good for this purpose because they are rich in tone and texture, while they go with most colors.

3. **Materials.** Another "tie" between the carport and house can be established by using the same or similar materials in the new structure. If the house roof is shingled, the same roofing on the carport would make both buildings "relatives." Here again, however, if you have established a strong enough tie between the carport and house through type and color, it may be all right to alter the materials used. For instance, a good wood carport would be a nice complement to a brick house—the materials work together very harmoniously—especially if the color is picked up and repeated in the carport.

BUILDING FREE-STANDING CARPORTS. Free-standing carports are constructed in the same manner as the attached carports described in Chapter 8. In fact, the only major difference is that one wall of a free-standing carport isn't fastened to the house as in the attached design. The basic carport consists of a slab, a series of supporting posts, and a roof. As you can see from the plans in this chapter, the roof design can be varied a great deal.

The slab. The construction of slabs for carports and garages given in Chapters 3, 6, and 8 holds good for free-standing carports, and, thus, there is no need for the subject to be discussed again. Nevertheless, it may be wise to say a few words about ordering and working with ready-mixed concrete—the fastest and easiest way to pour a slab or driveway (see Chapter 10).

To determine the amount of ready-mixed concrete you will need for a slab or driveway, figure out the area by multiplying the length (in feet) by the width (in feet). Then, to find out the number of cubic yards of concrete you'll need, divide the area by the factors given below:

If you want a thickness of:	Divide the area by:
3″	100
4″	75
5″	60
6″	50

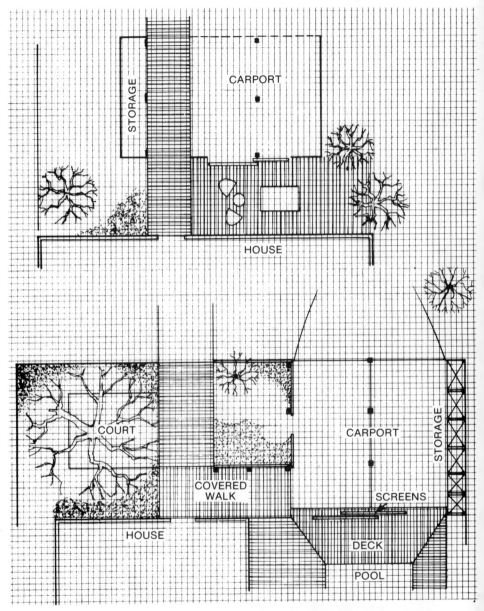

Top drawing is a plan for a limited area which demonstrates how easy it is to create useful space simply by carefully choosing the location of your carport. Between the carport structure and the house shown here, a patio or suncourt area is formed. Wise use of shrubbery and plantings will complete screening for privacy. Bottom drawing is an elaborate master plan for a great deal more outdoor activity to be developed around the carport. Included here are a garden spot, a shady court, storage, sundeck, and pool deck area. Note how the carport plays a major role in providing a screen against wind or for privacy. The use of gridded layout paper makes the job of laying out carports, garages, and driveways much easier.

These figures, by the way, include an extra 10 percent for any estimating errors.

As an example, let's say that you want a 4-inch thick carport slab and the area measures 22 feet wide by 22 feet long—a total area of 484 square feet. Divide 484 by 75 (you want a 4-inch slab, remember) and the answer is 6.45. You would order 6-1/2 cubic yards for the carport slab.

When placing an order for the slab concrete, be sure to specify a minimum of 6 sacks of cement per cubic yard and not more than 6 gallons of water per sack of cement. If you are placing concrete in cold weather—anything below 42 degrees F—ask the ready-mix producer either to use a high-early strength cement or to add calcium chloride to the mix. He probably will anyway, but you'll be sure to get what you want if you specify it. Concrete takes a longer time to harden in cold weather, and the use of either high-early strength cement or calcium chloride will speed up setting. Check the forms carefully to be sure they are as sturdy and rigid as possible. The wire mesh reinforcing should be placed 3/4 to 1 inch below the ultimate surface of the slab. Support the mesh on bricks or special "chairs" designed for this purpose.

Before the mix truck arrives, try to clear a path so the driver can back right up to the formwork. Avoid wheelbarrowing if you possibly can because it takes a great deal of time to unload a truck this way and you'll probably have to pay a holding charge if you keep the truck longer than a half hour. If the ground is muddy or the job really inaccessible, you will have to rely on wheelbarrows, but give this information to the plant so they can plan accordingly. Also, don't forget to check clearance on overhead wires, low branches, roof overhangs, and other possible obstructions. Know where oil or septic tanks are buried, and route the truck around these and other underground weak spots.

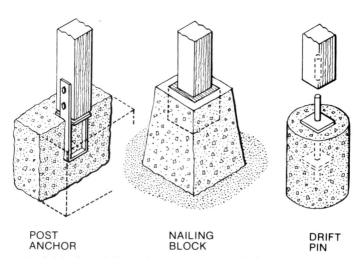

POST   NAILING   DRIFT
ANCHOR   BLOCK   PIN

If a concrete slab isn't used, the roof post supports can be fastened in any one of the methods shown above.

The tools needed for the concrete work—rake, shovel, strikeoff board, and trowels—as well as at least one helper should be on hand when the truck arrives. Always place concrete in the most distant part of the form first. However, before placing the first batch, wet the area down thoroughly so that the dry base will not suck moisture out of the concrete. It's best to do this several hours before the truck arrives. Place the concrete in the form in such a way that each load flows smoothly into the previous one, and place it so that you will have to make as little use of the rake and shovel as possible. As you move the concrete around, be sure to fill all the voids, particularly the areas along the sides of the form and around the reinforcing. Tap the sides of the form occasionally with the shovel to help settle the concrete.

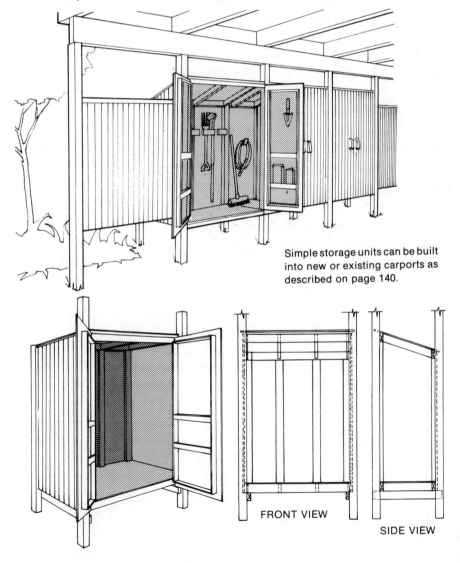

Simple storage units can be built into new or existing carports as described on page 140.

FRONT VIEW

SIDE VIEW

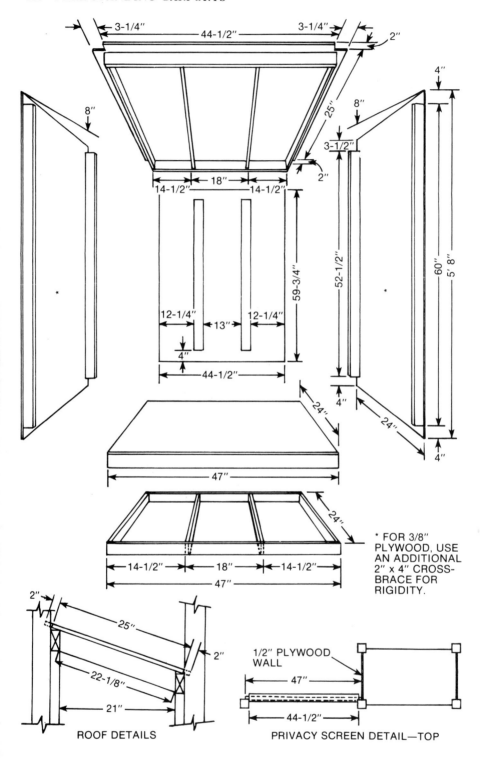

ROOF DETAILS

PRIVACY SCREEN DETAIL—TOP

* FOR 3/8"
PLYWOOD, USE
AN ADDITIONAL
2" x 4" CROSS-
BRACE FOR
RIGIDITY.

1/2" PLYWOOD
WALL

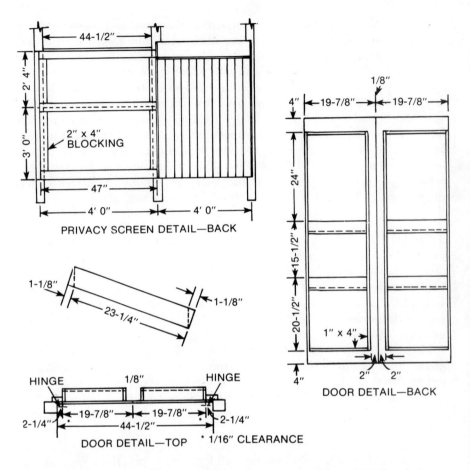

PRIVACY SCREEN DETAIL—BACK

HINGE

DOOR DETAIL—TOP   * 1/16" CLEARANCE

DOOR DETAIL—BACK

Construction details shown on facing page and above are for storage unit that can be used in either new or existing carports. Although vertical plywood has been shown, any suitable paneling may be substituted that will match decor of house.

When the form is completely filled, level the surface with a 2-by-4 strikeoff board. To accomplish this, put your helper on one of the strikeoff boards, which must be long enough to ride on top of the form across the newly poured concrete. With yourself on the other end, work the 2-by-4 back and forth in a saw-like motion. This is called screeding and gives a level and fairly smooth surface that is ready for floating or troweling. A couple of roof boards laid across the cement make a good platform from which to float or trowel. After the surface is smooth and the apron is tapered the way you want it, set in the anchor bolts or post base clips as indicated on your plan. Then, cover the concrete slab with a plastic polyethylene construction film or waterproof curing paper for several days. This will prevent the water in the concrete from evaporating too quickly while it is hardening.

The post and roof design. Most carports feature post and beam construction. This form has been used for years in barn building and recently in contemporary home design. It's a simple means of building—the posts are set on a slab, and they hold the beams onto which the roof is constructed. The posts are usually 4-by-4s, while the beams vary from 4-by-4s to 4-by-8s. Conventional 2-by-4 construction is used when building the storage areas, workshops, and play lofts. Any type of siding—it should complement the house, if possible—may be used for side walls and wind breaks or privacy screens. One of the most popular roofs for free-standing carports is a mopped-on hot-tar, built-up roof with a crushed stone or marble finish. However, this type of roof generally requires professional help. A built-up roll roof such as illustrated in Chapter 8 can also be used for free-standing carports.

STORAGE SPACE FOR EXISTING CARPORTS. If you have a *simple* carport—no storage space—it is possible to turn it into a multipurpose structure. Some of the storage ideas suggested for garages are given earlier in the book. Another method of providing storage is to install one or several shed-style plywood storage units between existing carport posts, with additional support from new posts at the rear of each unit. Privacy screens between the units give the carport a complete wall effect.

The dimensions given in the illustration of the shed storage unit may require alterations to suit the existing carport structure and individual storage requirements. To help in planning the latter, gather all the items you'll want to store in the shed(s); then determine the minimum dimension required to enclose all of them. Increase these dimensions by at least 1/4 to take care of any future needs.

To build a typical storage shed, proceed as follows:

1. Install the back 4-by-4 posts. Nail the 2-by-4-inch floor supports between the front and back posts on each side of the storage unit.

2. Build the walls, floor, and roof separately, using glue and finish nails spaced about 6 inches apart to fasten the plywood siding to the framing.

3. Set the floor in position and nail the floor framing to the floor supports and 4-by-4 posts, toenailing as necessary. Set the wall sections in place. Use the finish nails to nail through the plywood into the floor framing, and use 8d nails to nail the side framing to the posts. Install the roof, nailing the walls to the roof framing. Set the back in position and fasten to the walls and roof. Nail into the framing wherever possible.

4. Glue and nail the plywood door sections to the 1-by-4-inch framing. Install the hinges and hang the doors.

5. Apply the roofing. Finish the unit(s) with top-quality paints or stains according to the manufacturer's instructions. The colors should agree with or complement the carport.

6. Frame the screen section and fasten the plywood sections to it. You may wish to cover the horizontal butt joint with a decorative batten or a flashing piece, but this is optional.

10 | Plan Your Driveway Carefully

THE DRIVEWAY from the garage to the street should be planned to fit your lot. With a little extra thought, you may be able to include a turnaround plus off-street parking. Such a feature in your driveway adds safety, convenience, beauty, and additional value to your property.

In planning a driveway, there are several important items to take into consideration. For instance, the length and width of the vehicles using the driveway are prime factors in its layout. The widths of today's automobiles range from 4 to 7 feet, with the average full-size car being approximately 6 feet, 6 inches. In any case, the driveway should be 36 inches wider than the widest vehicle it will serve. Even if your present car is narrower than an average full-size vehicle, you should take into account the fact that your next automobile may be wider. Therefore, the minimum width of a driveway should be 8 feet, but preferably 9 feet or more. A 12-foot minimum width is necessary for curving drives.

An attractive driveway adds beauty to the garage and your home (Courtesy of Portland Cement Assoc.).

This unusual, but beautiful approach to a home's driveway combines exposed-aggregate concrete with redwood divider strips.

For a two-car garage or carport, a double width driveway is desirable. But, if the distance from the garage or carport to the street is great, a single drive may be built to within a few car lengths of the vehicle's home, then widened to some 18 to 24 feet. This will permit a car to swing easily into either parking area of the garage. Short driveways for two-car garages should be about 16 to 20 feet wide.

With a detached garage, it is a good idea, if possible, to provide for a turning area where you can turn around after you back out of the garage and so you'll not be required to back into the street. There's always an element of danger in backing out, particularly where children are around or where the driveway is curved or sloping. But, when providing space for turning, keep in mind that the rear wheels don't follow in the tracks of the front wheels. Because of this, the driveway must be wider on turns than on the straight sections. For the average turning radius, a minimum of 10 feet is usually recommended. It is advisable, however, to try turning your car in the planned space to be sure the area is large enough. Remember that the ease of driving depends mainly upon the uniformity of the driveway's curvature, while the speed permissible is dependent upon its width. Keep all plantings 2 feet back from the edges of the curves so that cars can overhang the drive at these spots.

The overall length of the vehicle—not the wheelbase—is an important consideration when planning an off-street parking area. The average American full-size car length is about 18 feet, although some of Detroit's larger, deluxe models approach 20 feet. On the other hand, some of the smaller cars are only about 10 feet. Thus, it's quite evident that there's a variance in the parking requirements of today's cars. But in most cases, it's best to figure your off-street parking on the larger vehicles.

One of the simplest ways of providing off-street parking is to widen the driveway on one or both sides. The amount of widening necessary will depend on the method of parking employed. For example, if you plan on parallel parking, the spaces should be approximately 8 feet wide and 22 feet long to permit safe maneuvering in and out. The driveway at that point should be 12 feet wide, making a total width of 20 feet.

Straight-in parking space usually needs a 9-foot minimum width, 18 feet of parking length, and 24 feet more for backing out. Sixty-degree angle-parking spaces should be at least 12 feet, 6 inches wide; this width is measured at right angles to the car. In addition, you'll require an 18-foot length for the car plus another 18 feet behind the vehicle for jockeying it in and out. As you can see, 60-degree angle-parking uses less space.

In addition to allowing for car size when planning your driveway, it's also a good idea to consider any alternate purposes for which it may be used. For instance, if there are children in the family, the driveway makes a good surface for a basketball court, a place to rollerskate, or an area for playing hopscotch. A driveway is also a good place to clean your car or do other tasks requiring a hard surface. And, if it is located near the patio or barbecue area, it may serve as a temporary entertainment spot. To help you plan your driveway, one of the eleven designs shown on pages 146 and 147 may serve as a thought-stimulator for you. Just remember, the dimensions shown should be considered minimum.

When laying out the driveway itself, make it as direct as possible. If feasible, locate it on the service side of the house for convenience to the side or rear entrances and for the delivery of household supplies. Unless service is needed to both sides of the house, it is not good to plan to have a driveway go around your home, since it's costly and it will break up the landscape design of most yards.

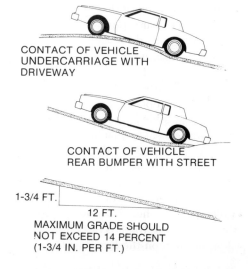

CONTACT OF VEHICLE UNDERCARRIAGE WITH DRIVEWAY

The driveway slope should be planned with gradual angles so car doesn't "bottom" on driveway or street.

CONTACT OF VEHICLE REAR BUMPER WITH STREET

1-3/4 FT.

12 FT.

MAXIMUM GRADE SHOULD NOT EXCEED 14 PERCENT (1-3/4 IN. PER FT.)

If the garage is considerably above or below street level and is located near the street, the driveway grade may be critical. A grade of 14 percent (1-3/4-inch vertical rise for each running foot) is the maximum recommended. The change in grade should be gradual to avoid scraping the car's bumper or underside. The most critical point occurs when the rear wheels are in the gutter as a vehicle approaches a driveway from the street.

If you're not sure how much grade there is between the proposed site of the garage and the street, you can get a good idea of what it is with an ordinary garden hose long enough to reach between the two places plus the help of another person. Fill the hose with water and have your helper take one end of it to the higher place, while you take the other end to the lower place. Meanwhile, each of you should hold a thumb over the hose ends to keep the water from running out. Have your helper hold his end of the hose exactly 1 foot off the ground. Hold your end up until you think it's about the same height as the other end. Take your thumb off the end of the hose and have your helper do the same thing. If water runs out of your end, your end is lower. If it runs out of his end, his end is lower. Your helper should have a can of water so that he can refill the hose, while you raise or lower your end until water stands clear to the top in both ends of the hose without running out. This means that both ends are at the same height. By measuring the height of your end of the hose from the ground and subtracting 1 foot (the distance the other end is off the ground), you can tell within a few inches how much lower the ground is where you stand.

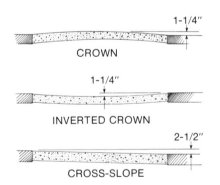

Methods of obtaining side drainage.

The driveway should be built with a slight slope so that it will drain quickly after a rain or washing. A slope of 1/4 inch per running foot is recommended. The direction of slope will depend on local conditions, but usually it should be toward the street. A crown or cross-slope may be used for drainage instead.

The part of a driveway between the street and public sidewalk is usually controlled by the local municipality. It should be consulted when a driveway is built after the street, curbs, and public walks are in place. If curb and gutter haven't been installed, it's advisable to end the driveway temporarily at the public sidewalk or property line. An entry of gravel or crushed stone can be

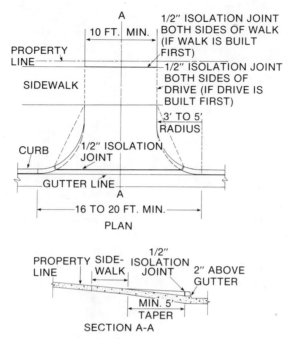

Details of a typical driveway entrance.

used until curbs and gutter are built. At that time, the drive entrance can be completed to meet local requirements. For better appearance, if possible, the street curb should be extended along the driveway up to the street sidewalk. Such a curb section should be curved to allow for easier turning into and out of the driveway. The width of the street also influences the amount of this turning radius.

DRIVEWAY CONSTRUCTION. There are three basic materials used today for driveways: (1) stone (gravel); (2) concrete; and (3) blacktop (asphalt). Each type of material has advantages and disadvantages.

Stone. A stone or gravel driveway is the most economical to install and thus is ideally suited for the long drives in suburban areas. They do tend to wash out and must have some type of curbing to keep the stone in place. Otherwise, the stone can work its way onto grass areas.

To construct a stone driveway, excavate to a depth of 8 inches below the grade surface. After installing the curbing—metal, brick, plastic, or wood—put a 6-inch layer of coarse stone or quarry shuck into the excavation and roll to compact it. To complete the job, place a 2-inch layer of fine crushed stone or gravel (from 1/4 to 1 inch in size) on the compacted stone base and roll it. The center of the road should be higher than the adjacent curbs so no water will stand on the surface of the road. That is, make the crown in the center of the driveway so that washout can be controlled to a degree.

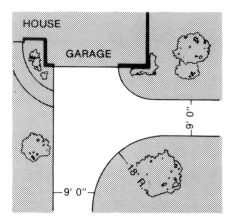

Entrance/exit for a narrow or wide corner lot.

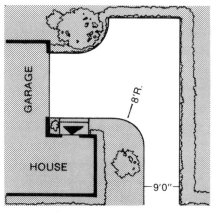

Garage, parking, turnaround at rear for wide lot.

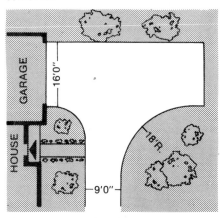

Garage at rear with side turnaround and parking for wide lot.

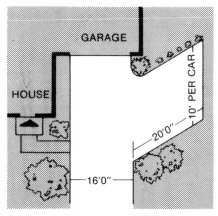

Garage, parking, turnaround at front for average lot.

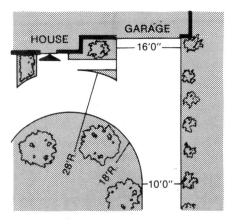

Garage at front with circle drive for narrow corner lot.

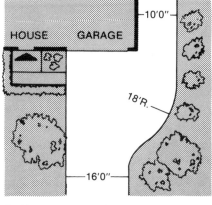

Parking, turnaround beside garage for narrow lot.

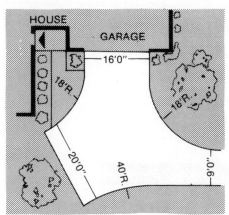

Garage, parking, turnaround at front for corner lot.

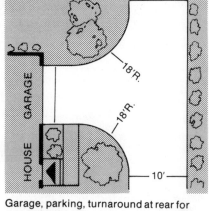

Garage, parking, turnaround at rear for corner lot.

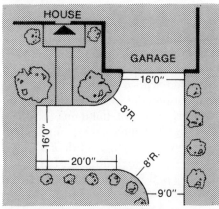

Garage, parking, turnaround at front for narrow lot.

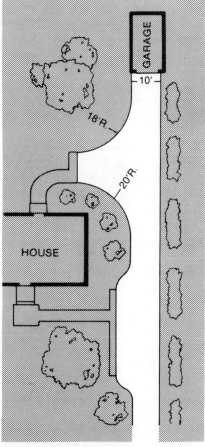

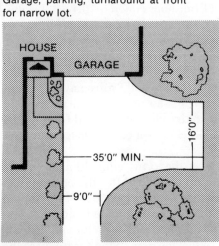

Garage, parking, turnaround at front for average lot.

Detached garage, parking, turnaround at rear for narrow lot.

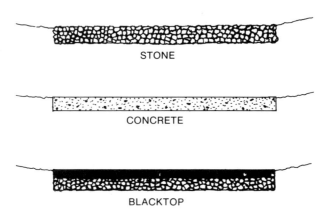

STONE

CONCRETE

BLACKTOP

The three basic types of driveways. Concrete and stone (gravel) are do-it-yourselfer material, while blacktop, because of equipment needed, is not.

Concrete. There are two styles of concrete driveways: (1) solid and (2) ribbon. The latter is the most economical of the concrete drives, but isn't very well suited for curved driveways. The solid drive is best for driving ease and maintenance. Both styles may be constructed with or without curbs. The thickness of the driveway depends primarily upon the weight of the vehicles that will use it. For passenger cars, 4 inches is sufficient; but if an occasional heavy truck uses the driveway, a thickness of 5 or 6 inches is recommended.

It is usually necessary to excavate the driveway area to a depth of 9 inches below the surface grade. Place a 3-inch layer of coarse stone on the bottom of the excavation. For a 4-inch driveway, 1-by-4 or 2-by-4-inch lumber may be used. Driveways of 6-inch thickness require at least 2-by-6-inch forms. Wood stakes are usually 1-by-2s, 1-by-4s, 2-by-2s, or 2-by-4s. Space stakes at 3- to 4-foot intervals. For ease in placing and finishing concrete, drive all stakes slightly below the top of the forms. Wood stakes can be sawed off flush. All stakes must be driven straight and true if forms are to be plumb.

Curves may be formed with 1-inch lumber, 1/4- to 1/2-inch thick plywood, hardboard, or sheet metal. Short-radius curves are easily obtained by bending plywood with the grain vertical. Two-inch thick wood forms may be bent to gentle horizontal curves during staking or to shorter-radius curves by saw kerfing. Wet lumber is easier to bend than dry lumber. To hold forms at the proper grade and curvature, set the stakes closer on curves than on straight runs.

Pour the concrete (1:2:3-1/2 mix) between the forms, embedding the mix in 1/2-inch round steel rods or heavy reinforced wire. After the concrete has been struck off and floated with a wood float, the area next to the form should be edged with a metal edger. This produces a neat, rounded edge that prevents chipping or damage, especially when the forms are removed. Edging also compacts and hardens the concrete surface next to the form where the float is less effective.

Driveways are seldom steel troweled; the wood float finish gives a desirable gritty, nonskid surface. Also, control joints—sometimes called expansion joints—should be spaced at an interval about equal to the driveway's width. Drives wider than 12 feet should have a longitudinal control joint down the center. Control joints help eliminate unsightly random cracks and are made with a tool called a jointer.

Another type of joint that's sometimes found in a driveway is the so-called "construction" joint. This is required where concreting operations are temporarily suspended, as at the end of a day's work. Construction joints should be avoided when possible; but, if necessary, they should be planned and located so as to act as control joints. A keyway is required to provide load transfer across a construction joint. This ensures that future slabs will remain level with previously cast concrete. The keyway may be formed by fastening

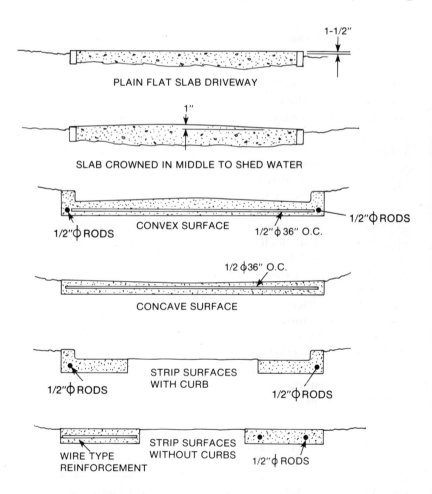

Typical concrete driveway sections.

metal, wood, or premolded key material to a wood bulkhead. Concrete above the joint should be hand tooled to match the control joints in appearance. Complete details on working with concrete can be found in the *Popular Science Skill Book*—HOW TO WORK WITH CONCRETE AND MASONRY.

Blacktop. Asphalt blacktop makes a good driveway, however, in very hot weather it tends to soften. Also, because of the equipment needed, most blacktop driveways are installed by a professional contractor.

The majority of blacktop driveways require 6 inches of coarse stone, 2 inches of fine crushed stone, and 2 to 3 inches of asphalt mix over this base. The driveway should be crowned in the center.

DRIVEWAY MAINTENANCE. All three driveway surfaces require some maintenance.

Stone. To keep driveways in top condition, it may be necessary every-so-often to fill surface holes and hollows with fine crushed stone. An occasional rolling with a heavy garden roller will keep the surface compacted. When making any repairs, be sure to maintain the crown in the center.

Concrete. Proper preparation of the damaged area is the key to successful concrete driveway repair. Chip away all cracked and crumbling areas. If the area is large, lightly tap out the damaged areas with an 8-pound sledge hammer. Be sure to remove all loose concrete, dust, dirt, loose paint, and other foreign materials down to a solid base.

If the area to be resurfaced requires an especially thin layer of new concrete, simply apply vinyl concrete patcher as directed on the package. A 40-pound bag will resurface approximately 20 square feet, 1/4 inch thick. For best results, apply a vinyl concrete patcher in applications of 1 inch thickness or less. If the required build-up is greater than 1 inch, apply it in layers and allow each layer to cure several days. For extra strength, use a concrete bonding adhesive as well.

Blacktop. To repair and seal a blacktop driveway, it is important to remove any loose asphalt to a depth of at least 2 inches, keeping the hole squared off with vertical sides or edges. Sweep out and clean the area to be filled. Apply a blacktop patch, building up 2 inches at a time. Compact the blacktop patch every 2 inches, using a tamper or garden roller, or by driving car wheels over the patch. No heating or mixing is required.

When finishing a patch, fill the material slightly higher than the surrounding area so that when the compacting is complete, the patch will be level with the surrounding area. A small amount of dry sand or cement sprinkled on the surface will speed hardening and eliminate tackiness. If the blacktop patch is hard to work, place it in a warm room until it is soft and pliable. Allow at least 36 hours before opening the driveway to heavy traffic and 5 days before applying the blacktop sealer.

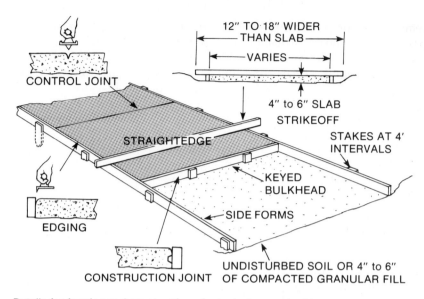

Details for forming and construction of a typical concrete driveway.

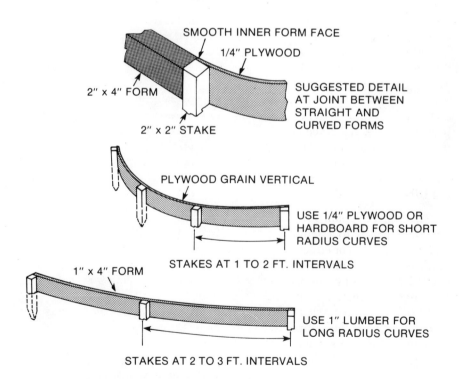

Details for forming horizontal curves.

After all chuckholes, cracks, and low areas have been repaired and all surfaces are firm, seal it with blacktop sealer. Clean all dirt, dust, oil, and gasoline from the pavement. Use a non-sudsing detergent directly on all gasoline and oil spots, scrubbing with a broom and completely flushing with water. Leave no puddles or excess water on the surface. Apply the blacktop sealer as directed, starting at the highest point and working to the lowest. Avoid heavy or uneven application. For average pavements, use two coats. For steep or slippery grades, mix silica sand with sealer for extra traction. Use 4 to 6 pounds of sand per gallon. Allow it to dry 24 hours before testing the surface for tackiness. **Note:** Coverage depends on the porosity and general condition of the old blacktop surface. Five gallons of a typical blacktop sealer will usually cover approximately 400-500 square feet. Second coat coverage can be 30 to 50 percent greater than the first coat. Allow new or freshly-laid blacktop to cure for a minimum of 30 days before sealing it. Coverage on new blacktop varies greatly.

The step-by-step procedure involved in making a driveway. The newly poured concrete can be cured by sealing the surface with plastic sheeting, waterproof paper, or curing compound, or by supplying water with wet coverings, sprinkling, or ponding. The purpose of curing is to prevent too much water from being lost to evaporation before the concrete has properly hardened.

Index

HOW TO BUILD YOUR GARAGE OR CARPORT
by Robert Scharff

This informative book contains complete information on building, adding on, or expanding garages, adding storage and work centers, adapting present garages to new living space, installing doors, paving driveways, and building carports. Early chapters explain with step-by-step photos how to build a new garage – either freestanding or attached to your house. There are many plans to choose from. There are chapters on how to expand your present garage, add storage facilities or useful features such as workbench, garden center, etc. There are details on how to convert a former garage to living space, how to buy and install a garage door, add an automatic garage door opener, how to plan and lay out a driveway. Two final chapters tell in text and photos how to build carports.

THE POPULAR SCIENCE SKILL BOOK SERIES

POPULAR SCIENCE SKILL BOOKS help sharpen the skill of the home handyman by providing practical, down-to-earth information from the top do-it-yourself experts. Uniform in size and style, each book provides a text that's clear, easy to follow and fully illustrated. Other POPULAR SCIENCE SKILL BOOKS include:

HOW TO DO YOUR OWN WOOD FINISHING by Jackson Hand

HOW TO BUILD YOUR CABIN OR MODERN VACATION HOME by Harry Walton

HOW TO USE HAND AND POWER TOOLS by George Daniels

HOW TO BE YOUR OWN HOME ELECTRICIAN by George Daniels

HOW TO BUILD FURNITURE by R. J. DeCristoforo

PLUMBING, HEATING AND AIR CONDITIONING by George Daniels

HOME AND WORKSHOP GUIDE TO SHARPENING by Harry Walton

HOW TO MAKE YOUR OWN RECREATION AND HOBBY ROOMS by Ralph Treves

HOW TO WORK WITH CONCRETE AND MASONRY by Darrell Huff

HOW TO DO YOUR OWN PAINTING AND WALLPAPERING by Jackson Hand

HOW TO BUILD PATIOS AND DECKS by Richard Day

HOME GUIDE TO LAWNS AND LANDSCAPING by Bruce Cassiday

HOMEOWNER'S QUICK-REPAIR AND EMERGENCY GUIDE by Max Alth

BASIC CAR MAINTENANCE AND REPAIRS by Paul Weissler

HOME GUIDE TO SOLAR HEATING AND COOLING by Jackson Hand

HEATING YOUR HOME WITH WOOD by Neil Soderstrom

HOW TO DO YOUR OWN HOME INSULATING by L. Donald Meyers

PLANNING AND BUILDING YOUR HOME WORKSHOP by David Manners

HOW TO REPAIR, RENOVATE AND DECORATE YOUR WALLS, FLOORS AND CEILINGS by Jackson Hand

REMODELING YOUR KITCHEN AND BUILDING YOUR OWN CABINETS by Virginia T. Habeeb and Ralph Treves

REMODELING YOUR BATHROOM by Patrick Galvin

PLANNING AND BUILDING YOUR HOME WORKSHOP by David Manners

HOW TO BUILD YOUR GARAGE OR CARPORT by Robert Scharff